SkillBuilder

Grade 4

English Workbook - 1

▸ *Reading: Literature*
▸ *Reading: Informational Text*

Complement Classroom Learning All Year

Using the Lumos Study Program, parents and teachers can reinforce the classroom learning experience for children. It creates a collaborative learning platform for students, teachers and parents.

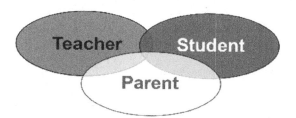

Used in Schools and Libraries To Improve Student Achievement

Developed by Expert Teachers

Contributing Author - Mary Evans Rumley
Contributing Author - Julie Turner
Executive Producer - Mukunda Krishnaswamy
Designer - Harini Nagaraj
Database Administrator - Raghavendra Rao R.

ISBN-10: 1-940484-89-8

ISBN-13: 978-1-940484-89-1

Printed in the United States of America

For permissions and additional information contact us

Lumos Information Services, LLC
Email: support@lumoslearning.com

PO Box 1575
Piscataway, NJ 08855-1575
Tel: (732) 384-0146
Fax: (866) 283-6471

http://www.LumosLearning.com

Lumos Reading Comprehension Skill Builder, Grade 4 - Literature, Informational Text and Evidence-based Reading

This Book Includes:

- Practice questions to help students master
  - ‣ Reading: Literature
  - ‣ Reading: Informational Text
- Detailed Answer explanations for every question
- Strategies for building speed and accuracy

Plus access to Online Workbooks which include:

- Instructional videos
- Mobile apps related to the learning objective
- Hundreds of additional practice questions
- Self-paced learning and personalized score reports
- Instant feedback after completion of the workbook

Table of Contents

Introduction

Books in the Lumos Skill Builder series are designed to help students master specific skills in Math and English Language Arts. The content of each workbook is rigorous and aligned with the robust standards. Each standard, and substandard, has its own specific content. Taking the time to study and practice each standard individually can help students more adequately understand and demonstrate proficiency of that standard in their particular grade level.

Unlike traditional printed books, this book provides online access to engaging educational videos, mobile apps and assessments. Blending printed resources with technology based learning tools and resources has proven to be an effective strategy to help students of the current generation master learning objectives. We call these books tedBooks™ since they connect printed books to a repository of online learning resources!

Additionally, students have individual strengths and weaknesses. Being able to practice content by standard allows them the ability to more deeply understand each standard and be able to work to strengthen academic weaknesses. The online resources create personalized learning opportunities for each student and provides immediate individualized feedback.

We believe that yearlong learning and adequate practice before the test are the keys to success on standardized tests. The books in the Skill Builder series will help students gain foundational skills needed to perform well on the standardized tests.

How to Use this Book Effectively

The Lumos Program is a flexible learning tool. It can be adapted to suit a student's skill level and the time available to practice. Here are some tips to help you use this book and the online resources effectively:

Students

- The standards in each book can be practiced in the order designed, or in the order of your own choosing.
- Answer all questions in each workbook.
- Use the online workbooks to further practice your areas of difficulty and complement classroom learning.
- Watch videos recommended for the lesson or question.
- Download and try mobile apps related to what you are learning.

Parents

- Get student reports and useful information about your school by downloading the Lumos SchoolUp™ app. Please follow directions provided in "How to download Lumos SchoolUp™ App" section of this chapter.
- Review your child's performance in the "Lumos Online Workbooks" periodically. You can do this by simply asking your child to log into the system online and selecting the subject area you wish to review.
- Review your child's work in each workbook.

- You can use the Lumos online programs along with this book to complement and extend your classroom instruction.
- Get a Free Teacher account by visiting http://lumoslearning.com/a/fta

This Lumos StepUp® Basic account will help you:

- Create up to 30 student accounts.
- Review the online work of your students.
- Create and share information about your classroom or school events.

NOTE: There is a limit of one grade and subject per teacher for the free account.

- Download the Lumos SchoolUp™ mobile app using the instructions provided in "How can I Download the App?" section of this chapter to conveniently monitor your students online progress.

How to Access the Lumos Online Workbooks

First Time Access:

Using a personal computer with internet access:

Go to http://www.lumoslearning.com/a/workbooks

Select your State and enter the following access code in the Access Code field and press the Submit button.

Access Code: NCG4LR-49951-P

Using a smartphone or tablet:

Scan the QR Code below and follow the instructions.

In the next screen, click on the "Register" button to register your username and password.

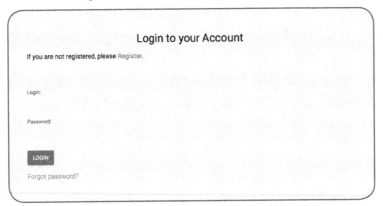

Subsequent Access:

After you establish your user id and password for subsequent access, simply login with your account information.

What if I buy more than one Lumos Study Program?

Please note that you can use all Online Workbooks with one User ID and Password. If you buy more than one book, you will access them with the same account.

Go back to the **http://lumoslearning.com/a/workbooks** link and enter the access code provided in the second book. In the next screen simply login using your previously created account.

4

Lumos StepUp® Mobile App FAQ For Students

What is the Lumos StepUp® App?

It is a FREE application you can download onto your Android smart phones, tablets, iPhones, and iPads.

What are the Benefits of the StepUp® App?

This mobile application gives convenient access to Practice Tests, Common Core State Standards, On-line Workbooks, and learning resources through your smart phone and tablet computers.

- Eleven Technology enhanced question types in both MATH and ELA
- Sample questions for Arithmetic drills
- Standard specific sample questions
- Instant access to the Common Core State Standards
- Jokes and cartoons to make learning fun!

Do I Need the StepUp® App to Access Online Workbooks?

No, you can access Lumos StepUp® Online Workbooks through a personal computer. The StepUp® app simply enhances your learning experience and allows you to conveniently access StepUp® Online Workbooks and additional resources through your smart phone or tablet.

How can I Download the App?

Visit **lumoslearning.com/a/stepup-app** using your smart phone or tablet and follow the instructions to download the app.

**QR Code
for Smart Phone
Or Tablet Users**

Lumos SchoolUp™ Mobile App FAQ For Parents and Teachers

What is the Lumos SchoolUp™ App?

It is a free app that teachers can use to easily access real-time student activity information as well as assign learning resources to students. Parents can also use it to easily access school-related information such as homework assigned by teachers and PTA meetings. It can be downloaded onto smart phones and tablets from popular App Stores.

What are the Benefits of the Lumos SchoolUp™ App?

It provides convenient access to
- Real-time student activity information.
- School "Stickies". A Sticky could be information about an upcoming test, homework, extra curricular activities and other school events. Parents and educators can easily create their own sticky and share with the school community.
- Discover useful educational videos and mobile apps.
- Common Core State Standards.
- Educational blogs.
- StepUp™ student activity reports.

How can I Download the App?

Visit **lumoslearning.com/a/schoolup-app** using your smartphone or tablet and follow the instructions provided to download the App. Alternatively, scan the QR Code provided below using your smartphone or tablet computer.

**QR Code
for Smart Phone
Or Tablet Users**

Reading Comprehension

The Elephant Who Saw the World

"The Elephant Who Saw the World," Mary started speaking. It was Friday, and the students had to share their creative writing stories of the week.

Mary loved writing, and this part of the week, when they were able to make up stories for creative writing, was her favorite part. She enjoyed it so much she became really good at it. When she was home on the weekends and she didn't have much homework, she would sit in her room for hours and create stories to share with her friends and family. Her parents always supported her and were her biggest fans.

However, there was one part about every Friday at school that Mary did not enjoy, and that was when she had to share her story in front of the class. The teacher made all of the children share on Friday afternoons, and this made Mary very nervous. She was shy, and although she knew her teacher was right, she didn't like it.

After sitting and listening to the other children share, Mary finally heard her name called. She knew it was her turn to share. She got out of her seat slowly, walked to the front of the room and began.

Question Number: 1   RL.4.1

What is the title of Mary's story?

Ⓐ   The Elephant Who Liked Candy
Ⓑ   The Elephant Who Saw the World
Ⓒ   The Elephant Who Wanted to See the World
Ⓓ   The Girl who Hated Writing

Question Number: 2   RL.4.1

What didn't Mary like doing?

Ⓐ   Writing stories and having others read them
Ⓑ   Having her stories corrected by the teacher
Ⓒ   Reading her stories in front of the class
Ⓓ   Going to school on creative writing days

Question Number: 3   RL.4.1

Why was Mary reading her story in front of the class?

Ⓐ   It was something she loved to do.
Ⓑ   Her classmates asked her to read her story.
Ⓒ   Every Friday the children had to share their creative writing stories.
Ⓓ   Her parents wanted her to practice.

Question Number: 4   RL.4.1

What do you think Mary did next?

Ⓐ Mary began running out of the classroom.
Ⓑ Mary began reading her story in front of the class.
Ⓒ Mary began to cry because she was scared.
Ⓓ Mary began to tell the teacher she didn't write a story.

Question Number: 5   RL.4.1

Why did Mary's parents support her love for writing stories?

Ⓐ so she wouldn't sit in front of the TV all day
Ⓑ to make sure she stayed busy
Ⓒ because she liked to write and was good at it
Ⓓ to make sure she kept her writing skills better than everyone else's

Question Number: 6   RL.4.2

Choose the sentence that best summarizes the passage.

Ⓐ The teacher required each student to read their story out loud.
Ⓑ They were presenting creative short stories as part of their Friday share time.
Ⓒ Though Mary loved creative writing, she did not enjoy reading her stories out loud.
Ⓓ Mary agreed that it would be good experience, but she still didn't like it.

Question Number: 7   RL.4.2

Which information is NOT necessary for the summary?

Ⓐ Mary enjoyed creating the stories, but when it came to presenting them, she got really nervous.
Ⓑ She enjoyed writing.
Ⓒ This was a strong point of hers.
Ⓓ Mary even wrote at home during her free time

Question Number: 8   RL.4.2

What would be the best summary for the passage above?

Ⓐ Mary wrote a story about an elephant who traveled the world. She loved writing
     stories and was excited when they had to do one for class. The teacher always asked
     the students to present their stories to the class during Friday share time. This was the
     part that Mary didn't like. She got really nervous speaking in front of the class al-
     though she knew it would be a good experience. When it was her turn, she took a
     deep breath and started sharing her story.

Ⓑ Mary wrote a story called "The Elephant Who Saw the World." Her family supported
     her passion for writing stories because she was so good at it. She was excited when
     the teacher assigned this for class one day.

Ⓒ "The Elephant Who Saw the World," Mary started speaking. It was Friday, and
     they had to share their creative writing stories of the week.
     Mary loved writing, and this was her favorite part of the week, when they were able
     to make up stories for creative writing. She enjoyed it so much that she became really
     good at it. Even at home on the weekends when she didn't have much homework,
     she would sit in her room for hours and create stories to share with her friends and
     family. Her parents always supported her and were her biggest fans.
     However, there was one part about every Friday at school that Mary did not enjoy,
     and that was when she had to share her story in front of the class. The teacher made
     all of the children share on Friday afternoons, and this made Mary very nervous. She
     was shy, and although she knew her teacher was right, she didn't like it.
     Sitting and listening to the other children, Mary heard her name called. It was her
     turn to share. She got out of her seat slowly, walked to the front of the room and
     began.

Ⓓ Mary loved writing stories. She wrote one about a donkey traveling the world and
     had to present it in front of the class. She was nervous about this.

Question Number: 9   RL.4.3

Where does the story take place?

- Ⓐ at Mary's house
- Ⓑ on the playground at school
- Ⓒ in Mary's classroom
- Ⓓ at a restaurant

Question Number: 10   RL.4.3

Which event in the above passage made Mary nervous?

- Ⓐ writing a story
- Ⓑ talking to the teacher
- Ⓒ sharing her work in front of the class
- Ⓓ showing her family what she had done

Question Number: 11   RL.4.7

Which picture below best represents what's happening in the story?

Ⓐ

Ⓑ

Ⓒ

Ⓓ **None of the above**

Alex the Great

Nearly two thousand five hundred years ago, there lived a king called Alexander the Great. He was the son of Philip II of Macedonia. When Alexander was a boy, a magnificent horse for sale was brought to the court of his father. The animal was to be sold for thirteen talents. Talents are ancient coins. Many were eager to buy the horse, but none could get close enough to saddle the restless animal. He was wild, and it was impossible to ride him.

Alexander pleaded with his father to let him try. Realizing that the horse was terrified of its own shadow, he turned the horse towards the sun so that its shadow fell behind it. This calmed the horse, and the prince proudly rode away. Observing this, his father said, "My son, look for a kingdom worthy of your greatness. Macedonia is too small for you."

That is exactly what Alexander tried to do when he grew up. He fought many battles and always rode Bucephalus (that was the horse's name.) Friendship and trust grew between man and horse. When Bucephalus died of wounds received in battle, Alexander was heartbroken and deeply mourned the loss of his horse. He wished that he had died along with it.

Question Number: 1   **RL.4.1**

How did Alexander calm the horse when he was for sale?

Ⓐ He saddled and rode him.
Ⓑ He talked in a soothing voice.
Ⓒ He pleaded with his father to let him try.
Ⓓ He turned the horse so he couldn't see his shadow.

Question Number: 2   **RL.4.1**

According to the passage, why do you think the horse was unrideable and wild?

Ⓐ because it was angry
Ⓑ because it was hungry
Ⓒ because it was scared
Ⓓ because it was good at riding

Question Number: 3   **RL.4.3**

When did this story take place?

Ⓐ two thousand five hundred years ago
Ⓑ two hundred and fifty years ago
Ⓒ twenty five hundred years ago
Ⓓ It is happening now.

Question Number: 4   **RI.4.2**

What is the main idea of this passage?

Ⓐ Alexander's love for animals
Ⓑ Alexander's smartness and greatness
Ⓒ Taming a wild horse
Ⓓ King Philip II

My Vacation in Hawaii

This year Jim and I had the most wonderful vacation compared to the one we took last year. We went to Hawaii, which is a much better place to visit than a hunting lodge in Alaska. The hotel we stayed in was a luxury suite; it included a big screen TV with all of the movie channels, a hot tub on the balcony, a small kitchen stocked with local fruits and vegetables, and a huge bed shaped like a pineapple. The weather in Hawaii could not have been any better. We enjoyed many hours on the beach sunbathing and playing volleyball. When we were not on the beach, we were in the ocean swimming or riding the waves on a surf board. Each night we enjoyed eating and dancing with all of our friends at a luau. Our week in Hawaii rushed by, making us wish we had planned a two-week vacation.

On the other hand, the hunting lodge in Alaska that we stayed in had a shower with hardly any warm water, a small cooler for our food, and cots to sleep on each night. But, the room wasn't even the worst part of the vacation. The weather was terrible; it rained the entire time we were there. Even with the rain, our guide expected us to go on the all-day fishing trip that was part of our vacation package. All we caught on that fishing trip was a cold from the rain. After the third day in Alaska, we decided to end our nightmare, cut our trip short, and head for home. Without a doubt, we will be going back to Hawaii next year on our vacation.

Question Number: 1   **RL.4.1**

Which statement supports the author's opinion that their Alaska vacation was miserable?

Ⓐ   Our week in Hawaii rushed by, making us wish we had planned a two-week vacation.
Ⓑ   The weather in Hawaii could not have been better.
Ⓒ   This year Jim and I had the most wonderful vacation compared to the one we took last year in Alaska.
Ⓓ   After the third day in Alaska, we decided to end our nightmare, cut our trip short, and head for home.

Question Number: 2   **RL.4.1**

Which statement supports the author's opinion that their Hawaii vacation was wonderful?

Ⓐ   "Our week in Hawaii rushed by, making us wish we had planned a two-week vacation."
Ⓑ   "The weather in Hawaii could not have been better."
Ⓒ   "This year Jim and I had the most wonderful vacation compared to the one we took last year in Alaska."
Ⓓ   "After the third day in Alaska, we decided to end our nightmare, cut our trip short, and head for home."

14

Question Number: 3   RL.4.1

Which detail describes where they stayed in their favorite vacation?

Ⓐ "The hunting lodge that we stayed in had no TV, a shower with barely warm water, a small cooler for our food, and cots to sleep on each night."
Ⓑ "It included a big screen TV with all of the movie channels, a hot tub on the balcony, a small kitchen stocked with local fruits and vegetables, and a huge bed shaped like a pineapple."
Ⓒ "The weather in Hawaii could not have been any better. We enjoyed many hours on the beach sunbathing and playing volleyball."
Ⓓ "When we were not on the beach, we were in the ocean swimming or riding the waves on a surf board. Each night we enjoyed eating and dancing with all of our friends at a luau."

Question Number: 4   RL.4.5

Choose the text structure used in this passage.

Ⓐ Cause and effect
Ⓑ Compare and contrast
Ⓒ Problem and solution
Ⓓ Sequence

Your science book might have a lesson of a boy who catches an illness from germs that are spread. He has to see a doctor who shows him how to keep from getting sick in the future.

Question Number: 5   RL.4.5

What is the structure of the above text?

Ⓐ Cause and effect
Ⓑ Compare and contrast
Ⓒ Problem and solution
Ⓓ Sequence or chronological

Question Number: 6   RL.4.9

Compare and contrast the Alaskan and Hawaiian vacations. Which statement is correct?

Ⓐ Both had beautiful hotel rooms with nice accommodations.
Ⓑ The weather in Alaska was beautiful, but it rained the entire time they were in Hawaii.
Ⓒ The Hawaiian vacation was much more enjoyable than the Alaskan vacation.
Ⓓ The Alaskan vacation was much more enjoyable than the Hawaiian vacation.

The Surprise Vacation

Before going to bed on Friday night, Susie's parents told her they had a surprise planned for the weekend and she would have to wake up really early on Saturday morning. When she woke up, they left the house quickly and started driving. While in the car, Susie looked outside to see if she could figure out where they were going. She noticed that it was getting really hot out and the sun was shining brightly. Then she noticed that the surfboards were in the car. Finally, they stopped, and Susie said, "I know where we are going!"

Question Number: 1   RL.4.1

What season is it?

Ⓐ Summer
Ⓑ Spring
Ⓒ Winter
Ⓓ Fall

Question Number: 2   RL.4.1

Where do Susie and her family probably live?

Ⓐ in Alaska
Ⓑ close to the beach
Ⓒ in the mountains
Ⓓ in Arkansas

Question Number: 3   RL.4.5

What is the structure of the text?

Ⓐ Cause and Effect
Ⓑ Problem and Solution
Ⓒ Sequencing and Chronological
Ⓓ Description

Fred Goes to the Dentist

Fred had never been to the dentist. All of his life he had heard horror stories about the buzzing drills, the huge needles, and the scary tools that the dentist used to torture his patients. Since none of his teeth were hurting, Fred just couldn't understand why his mom was insisting on taking him to see one. She told him that it was important to visit the dentist each year to have your teeth checked and to get your teeth cleaned. That was just silly to Fred since he cleaned his teeth everyday by brushing and flossing them, but nothing would change his mother's mind. He found it hard to believe that she would think it was a good idea to take him somewhere to be tortured. However, he had no choice but to go.

On the way to the dentist, Fred's imagination went wild. He pictured walking into a room with a huge chair that the dentist would strap him to. He could just see the dentist pulling out a huge drill and drilling his tooth while his mother and several others held him in the chair. By the time he got to the dentist's office, he was shaking all over.

To his surprise, the office was nothing like he expected. The dentist was nice, and the chair was comfortable and didn't have any straps with which to tie him to it. He looked around the room and didn't see any huge drills or torture devices. He was relieved when all the dentist did was look in his mouth, show him how to properly brush and floss his teeth, and give him a balloon. His mom made an appointment to have his teeth cleaned. Maybe this wouldn't be as bad as he had thought it would be.

Question Number: 1   RL.4.2

What is the theme of the above passage?

Ⓐ Dentists are good people so don't worry about seeing them.
Ⓑ Moms usually know best so trust them.
Ⓒ Things are usually not as bad as you think they will be.
Ⓓ Imagination is good but it can make things scary sometimes.

Question Number: 2   RL.4.3

Based on the above passage, how do you think Fred felt about going to his first visit to the dentist?

Ⓐ He was excited and looked forward to it.
Ⓑ He was afraid and didn't understand why he had to go.
Ⓒ He was afraid but wanted to go and see the drills.
Ⓓ He felt shy about meeting the dentist.

Question Number: 3   RL.4.3

How do you think Fred felt after seeing the dentist office and meeting the dentist?

(A) scared
(B) intimidated
(C) relieved
(D) joyful

Question Number: 4   RL.4.3

The setting for the second paragraph of the above passage is probably:

(A) the dentist's office
(B) an automobile
(C) fred's home
(D) school

Question Number: 5   RL.4.3

Which detail shows that Fred is worried about going to the dentist?

(A) "To his surprise, the office was nothing like he expected."
(B) "Since none of his teeth were hurting, Fred just couldn't understand why his mom
     was insisting on taking him to see one."
(C) "By the time he got to the dentist he was shaking all over."
(D) "Maybe this wouldn't be as bad as he thought it would be."

Question Number: 6   RL.4.3

What did Fred imagine was going to happen to him at the dentist office?

(A) The dentist would pull a tooth and then give him a balloon.
(B) The dentist would tie him to the chair and use a huge drill on him.
(C) His mother would hold him down, and the dentist would clean his teeth.
(D) The dentist would tie him down and floss his teeth.

Question Number: 7   RL.4.3

What actually happened at the dentist office?

Ⓐ The dentist showed him how to brush and floss his teeth.
Ⓑ The dentist pulled a tooth.
Ⓒ The dentist drilled his tooth.
Ⓓ The dentist pulled a tooth and gave him a balloon.

Question Number: 8   RL.4.9

Compare the way Fred felt about going to the dentist before his visit to the way he felt after his first visit.

Ⓐ Fred was excited about going but became afraid once he arrived.
Ⓑ Fred was afraid of going and was even more afraid after he met the dentist.
Ⓒ Fred was afraid of going but felt relieved after he met the dentist.
Ⓓ Fred was excited about going and loved it once he arrived.

NOTES

Honesty is the Best Policy

Opal walked into the store not wanting to do what she had planned. She knew when she took the makeup without paying for it that it was wrong. She felt so guilty. She knew she couldn't keep the makeup. So, gathering all of her courage, she walked up to the security officer and confessed what she had done. He admonished her for shoplifting but let her off with a warning because she had been honest. She felt very relieved.

Question Number: 1   RL.4.2

What is the theme of the above passage?

Ⓐ   The unknown can be scary.
Ⓑ   It is best to be honest.
Ⓒ   Don't cry over spilled milk.
Ⓓ   Mom knows best.

Question Number: 2   RL.4.2

Summarize the above text using only one sentence.

Ⓐ   Opal was ashamed of what she did, so she returned it.
Ⓑ   Opal stole some makeup; however, she returned it because she felt guilty.
Ⓒ   Opal walked to the store, and she returned the make-up.
Ⓓ   Open walked to the store and gathered her courage, because she stole some makeup.

Question Number: 3   RL.4.6

The above passage uses which style of narration?

Ⓐ   First person
Ⓑ   Second person
Ⓒ   Third person
Ⓓ   Fourth person

The Christmas Gift

Libby's grandmother didn't have much money, so she couldn't buy Libby an expensive present for Christmas like her other grandmother could. She didn't want to buy her some cheap toy that wouldn't last long, but she just couldn't afford the things that were on Libby's wish list. She decided that she would make Libby a quilt. She was afraid her granddaughter wouldn't like the gift, but it was the best that she could do.

When Christmas day arrived, Grandmother went to Libby's house. She saw all of the nice gifts that her granddaughter had received. She was worried as Libby began to open her present. Libby squealed with delight when she saw the handmade quilt. She ran and hugged her grandmother and thanked her. She ran and put the new quilt on her bed. The rest of the day she talked about how much she loved the quilt, especially since her grandmother had made it all by hand.

Question Number: 1   RL.4.2

What is the theme of the above passage?

Ⓐ It is not the cost of the gift that matters but the thought and love put into it.
Ⓑ Expensive gifts are better than homemade ones.
Ⓒ Homemade gifts are as good as expensive toys.
Ⓓ Good manners have positive results.

Question Number: 2   RL.4.2

Which of the following is NOT the theme of this passage?

Ⓐ It's not the cost of the gift that matters.
Ⓑ Expensive gifts are better than homemade ones.
Ⓒ A gift from the heart is valuable.
Ⓓ A gift made with love is the best gift of all.

Question Number: 3   RL.4.3

How would you describe the way Libby's grandmother felt before Libby opened her gift?

Ⓐ nervous
Ⓑ kind
Ⓒ lazy
Ⓓ angry

Question Number: 4   **RL.4.3**

How do you think Libby's grandmother felt after Libby opened the gift?

Ⓐ sad
Ⓑ hungry
Ⓒ angry
Ⓓ happy

The Dental Nightmare

I was so scared when I first learned that I would be having my tooth pulled. I didn't sleep at all the night before the procedure. I was terrified that it would hurt more than I could bear. I was shaking like a leaf when I sat in the dentist chair. He promised me that it would not hurt, but I certainly had my doubts. The dentist then gave me some medicine. When I awoke, my tooth was gone and I didn't remember a thing.

Question Number: 1   RL.4.2

Choose the best summary of the above text.

Ⓐ   The writer was scared about having to have a tooth pulled and thought it would hurt. The dentist gave her medicine, and she didn't feel it when her tooth was pulled.
Ⓑ   The writer was scared. She got her tooth pulled. The dentist gave her medicine.
Ⓒ   The dentist gave the writer some medicine so that it wouldn't hurt when her tooth was pulled.
Ⓓ   The writer was scared about having her tooth pulled. She didn't sleep the night be fore. She was terrified. She was shaking like a leaf. The dentist gave her medicine. She didn't feel a thing when he pulled her tooth.

Question Number: 2   RL.4.6

The above passage uses which style of narration?

Ⓐ   First person
Ⓑ   Second person
Ⓒ   Third person
Ⓓ   Fourth person

Huckleberry Hound

Huckleberry Hound ran through the yard and into the field next to his house. Suddenly, he put his nose to the ground and started sniffing as he walked. Yep, he definitely smelled a rabbit. He raised his head and howled loudly to let the other dogs know what he had found. Then, he shot after the rabbit like a bolt of lightning. He chased that rabbit for what seemed like hours, but he never caught it. He returned to his yard with his head hanging and his tail tucked between his legs.

Question Number: 1   **RL.4.2**

Choose the best summary of the above text.

(A) Huckleberry Hound smelled a rabbit. He chased it for a long time, but never caught it.

(B) Huckleberry Hound smelled a rabbit. He ran across the yard to the field. He howled so the other dogs would know he found a rabbit. He shot after the rabbit and chased it for a long time. He didn't catch the rabbit. He went home with his head hung down.

(C) Huckleberry Hound chased a rabbit.

(D) Huckleberry Hound smelled a rabbit. He put his nose to the ground and followed its trail. He definitely smelled a rabbit. He chased it for a long time. He let the other dogs know he had found a rabbit. He didn't catch the rabbit.

Question Number: 2   **RL.4.6**

The above passage uses which style of narration?

(A) First person
(B) Second person
(C) Third person
(D) Fourth person

Oops! My Icecream!

I had been craving chocolate ice cream all day. Finally, school was over and I could go get a huge cone of chocolate ice cream. The line was long, but it was worth the wait. The first taste of my ice cream cone was delicious. Then, the worst thing imaginable happened. I bumped into the person behind me and dropped my ice cream on the floor.

Question Number: 1   RL.4.2

Summarize the above text using one sentence.

Ⓐ   I craved ice cream all day, but when I finally got a cone I dropped it on the floor.
Ⓑ   I craved ice cream all day, but I dropped it.
Ⓒ   I bought chocolate ice cream, and I bumped into someone and dropped it.
Ⓓ   The first taste of ice cream was great because I had been craving it all day.

Question Number: 2   RL.4.3

Where was the writer of the above passage while she was craving chocolate ice cream?

Ⓐ   at home
Ⓑ   at school
Ⓒ   at work
Ⓓ   at the mall

Question Number: 3   RL.4.3

Where was the writer when she dropped her ice cream on the floor?

Ⓐ   at the ice cream shop
Ⓑ   in the park
Ⓒ   in her car
Ⓓ   at home

Question Number: 4   RL.4.6

The above passage uses which style of narration?

Ⓐ   First person
Ⓑ   Second person
Ⓒ   Third person
Ⓓ   Fourth person

Bee Attack

It was a beautiful day outside, and a group of children were playing in the yard of one boy's house. They noticed a bee's nest up on the roof, so they started throwing rocks, sticks, and other items trying to knock it down. The nest moved a little, but it didn't fall to the ground. Instead, hundreds of bees flew out going everywhere.

Robert turned and ran away as fast as he could while yelling, "Get down! Get down!" He could hear Louise screaming. Robert dove to the ground as many bees flew over him. He could hear all the other kids doing the same.

The bee's nest was still hanging. John looked around the yard for something really long to use. He noticed his dad's rake sitting by the porch, so he took the rake and ran over to the porch. He swung it as hard as he could, hitting the nest. The nest was dislodged, went flying through the air, and landed near Robert. With a shriek, Robert jumped to his feet and ran to the other side of the yard. The others were also yelping and trying to run away.

Question Number: 1   **RL.4.2**

What is the best summary for the passage above?

Ⓐ John continued throwing things at the nest even after his friends were laying on the ground.

Ⓑ John wanted to destroy a bees' nest with his friends. They destroyed it and had to try and escape when the bees came flying out of it. Everyone was scared.

Ⓒ John and his friends were planning to destroy a bees' nest. They started throwing rocks and sticks at the nest. When all the bees started flying out of the nest, the kids started to run trying to escape the bees. The nest was still hanging from the porch so John went and knocked it off using a rake. It landed near Robert who got up really fast and ran to the other side of the yard.

Ⓓ John and his friends prepared to destroy a bees' nest. They threw sticks and stones at the nest to knock it off the porch. It didn't work, so John had to do it again. The nest went flying towards Robert who got scared and ran to the other side of the yard.

Question Number: 2   RL.4.2

Which sentence is NOT necessary for the summary?

Ⓐ He noticed his dad's rake sitting by the porch.
Ⓑ The kids wanted to destroy a bees' nest.
Ⓒ John and his friends tried to run from the bees that came flying out of their nest when the kids hit it.
Ⓓ Robert yelled, "Get down! Get down!"

Question Number: 3   RL.4.3

Where does the story take place?

Ⓐ near a lake
Ⓑ outside in the yard
Ⓒ in the basement of the house
Ⓓ at the school

Timothy

Timothy is a student at my school. He is well-liked by all of the teachers and students. We all know that we can count on Timothy to keep our secrets, to help us if we ask, and to always be on time. We know that he is always honest and expects others to be honest as well.

Last summer, Timothy got a job walking dogs each morning. When school started this year, everyone encouraged him to quit his job, but he decided to keep it. He knew it would be hard to get up every morning at 5 a.m. in order to get all of the dogs walked and then go to school all day. In addition, he planned to sing in the chorus, play basketball, and be a mentor in the tutoring program this year. He knows it will not be easy, but he thinks his hard work will be worth it. He is trying to save enough money to go to a youth camp next summer.

Question Number: 1   **RL.4.3**

According to the above passage, which set of adjectives would you choose to describe Timothy?

Ⓐ   Responsible and depressed
Ⓑ   Trustworthy and thoughtless
Ⓒ   Responsible and ambitious
Ⓓ   Arrogant and unfriendly

Question Number: 2   **RL.4.3**

Based on the above passage, what do you think Timothy would do if someone asked him to help them cheat on a test?

Ⓐ   help them cheat but ask them not to tell anyone
Ⓑ   tell them that cheating is dishonest and encourage them not to do it
Ⓒ   help them cheat because he doesn't want them to make a bad grade
Ⓓ   tell them to ask someone else to help them cheat.

Question Number: 3   **RL.4.3**

According to the above passage, Timothy is saving his money for what upcoming event?

Ⓐ   a football game
Ⓑ   a chorus trip
Ⓒ   youth camp
Ⓓ   a basketball game

Question Number: 4   **RL.4.3**

Timothy gets up at 5 a.m. every morning to:

- Ⓐ oractice basketball
- Ⓑ walk dogs
- Ⓒ do his homework
- Ⓓ tutor a classmate

The Two Brothers

Adam lives with his dad and his older brother Stanley. Adam and Stanley share a room. Most of the time Adam enjoys sharing a room with his brother, but there are times that he wished he had his own room. Being brothers, they have a lot in common; however, they are different in many ways.

Adam likes to spend time with his friends. If he is not with them, he is texting them or playing games with them online. Adam is always busy. He cannot stand to sit around and do nothing. In fact, the only time he is still is when he is sleeping. Adam plays football, basketball, soccer, and baseball. He loves to be involved in whatever is going on at school or at the town's youth center. He spends a lot of his time encouraging people to recycle and even volunteers at the youth center. Although he loves spending time with his friends, he is willing to give up time with them to help others.

Stanley, on the other hand, loves to stay at home. He enjoys activities that can be done alone such as reading, drawing, and spending time with his dogs. Most days after school you can find him at home enjoying one of his favorite activities. He also thinks recycling is important and makes sure his family does it. Although he likes being alone, he enjoys volunteering at the youth center with his brother. He thinks it is important to make a difference in the lives of others, which is why he thinks he would like to be a doctor. Adam and Stanley may be different in many ways, but they join together and make a difference in their community.

Question Number: 1   RL.4.3

Choose the set of words that best describes Stanley.

Ⓐ Solitary and caring
Ⓑ Rude and outgoing
Ⓒ Selfish and quiet
Ⓓ Solitary and rude

Question Number: 2   RL.4.3

Based on the passage, how do you think Adam and Stanley feel about one another?

Ⓐ They like and respect one another.
Ⓑ They do not like to spend time together.
Ⓒ They do not enjoy one another's company.
Ⓓ Adam is jealous of Stanley.

Question Number: 3   RL.4.3

Choose the set of words that best describes Adam.

- Ⓐ Friendly and greedy
- Ⓑ Thoughtful and outgoing
- Ⓒ Unhappy and mean
- Ⓓ Outgoing and greedy

Question Number: 4   RL.4.3

According to the passage above, what do Adam and Stanley enjoy doing together?

- Ⓐ Playing football
- Ⓑ Drawing cartoons
- Ⓒ Playing video games
- Ⓓ Volunteering at the youth center

NOTES

Weekend Vacation

"Dad and I need to go out of town this weekend," said Mom. "We'll be back on Monday, so the three of you are going to spend the weekend with your two aunts. "

Lindsay, Scarlet, and Austin loved their aunts and were really excited. They ran upstairs and started getting their things together to take with them. They put everything in one bag that they would have to take to school with them. They were going to stay with Aunt Margaret for two nights and the last night with their Auntie Josephine.

At the end of the school day, the children came running out of classroom doors from all different directions. Aunt Margaret was waiting for her nieces and nephew at the entrance to the school. She was wearing a bright red suit with a sparkly cat pin on it. She also had on a proper wool hat to match. She noticed a scuff on her shoes when her nieces and nephew ran up to her.

She cried, "Oh, my goodness! I am so happy you are here. The children at your school are just a bunch of hooligans. I was nearly trampled while I was standing here! Let's go get in the car." Aunt Margaret pointed to a large, green four-door station wagon parked in the lot.

Question Number: 1   RL.4.3

Where does the end of the story take place?

Ⓐ outside in the yard
Ⓑ in the children's bedroom
Ⓒ at the children's school
Ⓓ at Aunt Margaret's house

Question Number: 2   RL.4.3

What most likely happened to Aunt Margaret while she was waiting for her nieces and nephew?

Ⓐ The children ambushed her while she was waiting in the parking lot.
Ⓑ She was in a bad mood already and called the children "hooligans" for no reason.
Ⓒ Mean spirited children knocked her down because she was a stranger.
Ⓓ The school children were excited school was out and they bumped into her in their hurry to get to their homes and after school activities.

Question Number: 3   RL.4.3

Why did the children need to stay with their two aunts?

Ⓐ Their parents needed to hang decorations around the house.
Ⓑ Their parents were celebrating their anniversary.
Ⓒ Their parents needed to go out of town.
Ⓓ Their parents needed to help their little brother Austin go shopping for school.

Question Number: 4   RL.4.5

What is the structure of the above text?

Ⓐ a play
Ⓑ a comedy
Ⓒ a poem
Ⓓ a narrative

Shopping Frenzy

One day James went to town to buy new clothes. First, he tried on a pair of trousers. He didn't like the trousers, so he gave them back to the shopkeeper. Then, he tried on a robe which had the same price as the trousers. James was pleased with the robe, and he left the shop. Before he climbed on his donkey to ride home, the shopkeeper and the shop-assistant ran out.

Question Number: 1   RL.4.5

What is the structure of the above text?

- Ⓐ Descriptive
- Ⓑ Problem and Solution
- Ⓒ Cause and Effect
- Ⓓ Sequencing and Chronological

Question Number: 2   RL.4.6

What style of narration is the above text?

- Ⓐ First person
- Ⓑ Second person
- Ⓒ Third person
- Ⓓ Fourth person

Water, Water Everywhere but not a Drop to Drink!

Beatrice was so excited. This was truly a special day for her. She looked down and saw that her cup was sparkling with clean and cold water. She couldn't believe it was real! She had never seen water like that before. Slowly, she took a sip and it tasted so fresh. Her mother always told her how important water is.

The only way that Beatrice was able to get her water in the past was from the dirty water in a ditch not far from her home. Or, they would have to walk for miles to reach other areas that had water. The water wasn't very clean in the other areas, either. In fact, most of the time, this water had a horrible smell and was murky in color. Beatrice and her family knew it wasn't great but they didn't have any choice. The water that they drank was unclean, making Beatrice feel sick often.

Question Number: 1   RL.4.9

How did Beatrice get her water in the past?

Ⓐ They have always gotten their water from a faucet in their kitchen.
Ⓑ They used to get it from the well.
Ⓒ They used to get it from the dirty stream.
Ⓓ None of the above

Question Number: 2   RI.4.4

How would you explain the phrase "murky in color"?

Ⓐ vague and confused
Ⓑ bright and clear
Ⓒ obscure and thick with mist
Ⓓ dark, dingy, and cloudy

The Ostrich

The ostrich is the largest bird in the world, but it cannot fly. Its legs are so strong and long that it can travel faster by running. Ostriches use their wings to help them gather speed when they start to run. They also use them as brakes when turning and stopping.

Ostriches have been known to run at a rate of 60 miles an hour. This is faster than horses can run and as fast as most people drive cars.

These huge birds stand as tall as a horse and sometimes weigh as much as 298 pounds. In their home country of Africa, they are often seen with some of the larger animals. The zebra, which is also a fast runner, seems to be one of their favorite companions.

An ostrich egg weighs one pound, which is as much as two dozen chicken eggs. Ostrich eggs are delicious and are often used for food by people in Africa. The shells are also made into cups and beautiful ornaments.

Question Number: 1   **RI.4.1**

Why is it a good thing that the Ostrich can run, rather than fly?

Ⓐ The Ostrich does not enjoy flying.
Ⓑ The Ostrich is able to fly.
Ⓒ The Ostrich does not want to fly.
Ⓓ The Ostrich can travel faster by running.

Question Number: 2   RI.4.1

Devon says that Ostriches are shy and solitary birds. Which detail in the text proves him wrong?

Ⓐ "Ostrich eggs are delicious and are often used for food by people in Africa."
Ⓑ "An ostrich egg wieghs one pound."
Ⓒ "These huge birds stand as tall as a horse."
Ⓓ "The zebra, which is also a fast runner, seems to be one of their favorite companions."

Question Number: 3   RI.4.2

What is the main idea of the passage?

Ⓐ Ostriches are great because their eggs are delicious.
Ⓑ The ostrich is the largest bird with many interesting characteristics.
Ⓒ The ostrich is the largest bird but it cannot fly.
Ⓓ The ostrich lives in Africa.

Question Number: 4   RI.4.2

Which detail supports the main idea of the passage?

Ⓐ Ostriches are great because their eggs are delicious.
Ⓑ The ostrich is the smallest bird and can run very fast.
Ⓒ The ostrich is the largest bird that can fly very fast.
Ⓓ The ostrich lives in Africa.

The Blue Whale

The blue whale is quite an amazing creature. It is a mammal that lives its entire life in the ocean. The size of its body is also amazing. This whale can grow up to 98 feet long and weigh as much as 200 tons. It is the largest known animal to have ever existed. Its body is long and elegantly tapered, unlike other whales which have a rounder, stockier build. The way they are built, along with their extreme size, gives them a unique look. It also gives them the ability to move more gracefully and at greater speeds than you might think. Normally they travel around 12 mph, but they slow to 3.1 mph when feeding. They can even reach speeds up to 31 mph for short periods of time! Although they are extremely large animals, they eat small shrimp-like creatures called krill. Since the krill are so small, the blue whale eats about four tons daily as they swim deep in the ocean.

Blue whales do not live in tight-knit groups called pods like other whales. Instead, they live and travel alone or with one other whale. While traveling through the ocean, they come to the top to breathe air into their lungs through blowholes. They come from under the ocean, spitting water out of their blowhole. Then they roll and reenter the water with a grand splash of their large tail. They make loud, deep, and rumbling low-frequency sounds that travel great distances. This allows them to communicate with other whales as far as 100 miles away. Their cries can be felt as much as heard. This resonating call makes them the loudest animal on Earth. If you ever have the opportunity to see or hear a blue whale, it will be an experience you will not soon forget

Question Number: 1   **RI.4.1**

Angel argues that the blue whale is a solitary creature. What evidence from the text best supports his point?

Ⓐ   "Blue whales do not live in tight-knit groups called pods like other whales.
     Instead, they live and travel alone or with one other whale."
Ⓑ   "This whale can grow up to 98 feet long and weigh as much as 200 tons.
      It is the largest known animal to have ever existed."
Ⓒ   "They make loud, deep, and rumbling low-frequency sounds that travel great
     distances. This allows them to communicate with other whales as far as
     100 miles away."
Ⓓ   "Although they are extremely large animals, they eat small
     shrimp-like creatures called krill."

Question Number: 2   RI.4.3

How do blue whales breathe?

Ⓐ They use their blowholes to process oxygen found at deep ocean depths.
Ⓑ They spit water out of their blowholes and then rise to the surface to breathe air.
Ⓒ They rise to the surface, spit water out of their blowholes, and then breathe air in through their blowholes.
Ⓓ They roll and reenter the water with a grand splash of their large tail.

Question Number: 3   RI.4.3

How are blue whales able to communicate with other whales from great distances away?

Ⓐ They make a loud, deep, low frequency sound that is able to travel as much as 100 miles under water.
Ⓑ They use tiny whale telephones.
Ⓒ They send a high frequency sound that only other whales are able to hear.
Ⓓ Their cries can be heard but never felt.

Question Number: 4   RI.4.4

What is the meaning of the word resonating?

Ⓐ low
Ⓑ loud
Ⓒ silent
Ⓓ quiet

Question Number: 5   RI.4.5

The author used which text structure when writing this passage?

Ⓐ Problem and solution
Ⓑ Cause and effect
Ⓒ Sequence
Ⓓ Descriptive

Question Number: 6   RI.4.5

A report that explains how animal cells and plant cells are alike and how they are different would be written using which of the text structures?

Ⓐ Cause and effect
Ⓑ Compare and contrast
Ⓒ Problem and solution
Ⓓ Sequence or chronological

Question Number: 7   RI.4.7

What would be an important illustration or picture to include with this article?

Ⓐ a picture of the ocean
Ⓑ a picture of a pod of whales
Ⓒ a picture of an adult blue whale
Ⓓ a picture of a whaling ship

Question Number: 8   RI.4.8

Which statement did the writer of this passage use to support his opinion that the size of a blue whale's body is amazing?

Ⓐ The blue whale is quite an extraordinary creature.
Ⓑ Its body is long and elegantly tapered, unlike other whales which have a rounder, stockier body.
Ⓒ This whale can grow up to 98 feet long and weigh as much as 200 tons, making it the largest known animal to have ever existed.
Ⓓ Their build, along with their extreme size, gives them a unique appearance and the ability to move gracefully and at greater speeds than one might imagine.

Question Number: 9   RI.4.8

What evidence does the author provide in the second paragraph that supports the fact that whales communicate with one another?

Ⓐ Blue whales live and travel alone or with one other whale.
Ⓑ They emerge from the ocean, spewing water out of their blowhole, roll over, and re-enter the water with a grand splash of their tail.
Ⓒ They make loud, deep, and rumbling low-frequency sounds that travel great distances, which allow them to communicate with other whales as much as 100 miles away.
Ⓓ Their cries can be felt as much as heard.

The End of the Dinosaurs

Have you ever thought about what happened to the dinosaurs that once roamed the Earth? Well, scientists have developed several ideas through the years. One idea is that a giant meteorite crashed into our planet and caused a huge dust cloud to cover the Earth. The dust cloud was so enormous that it kept the sun's rays from reaching Earth. This caused all of the plants to die. With nothing to eat, the herbivores died. Because of this, the large carnivores also died, leaving the planet with no dinosaurs.

Question Number: 1   RI.4.1

Amelia asserts that dinosaurs definitely died because a giant meteorite crashed into Earth. What key words from the text would help Terrance to make a counter point?

Ⓐ "One such idea…"
Ⓑ "…a giant meteorite crashed into our planet"
Ⓒ "…leaving the planet with no dinosaurs."
Ⓓ This caused all of the plants to die.

Question Number: 2   RI.4.2

Which detail supports the idea that scientists believe a meteorite crashed into the planet and killed off the dinosaurs?

Ⓐ Scientists have developed several ideas through the years.
Ⓑ Have you ever thought about what happened to the dinosaurs that once roamed the Earth?
Ⓒ The dust cloud was so enormous that it kept the sun's rays from reaching Earth.
Ⓓ Leaving the planet with no dinosaurs.

Question Number: 3   RI.4.4

What is the meaning of the word herbivore?

Ⓐ a type of plant
Ⓑ an animal that eats only plants
Ⓒ a type of storm
Ⓓ an animal that eats only meat

Question Number: 4   **RI.4.4**

What is the meaning of the word carnivores?

(A) a type of plant
(B) an animal that eats only plants
(C) a type of storm
(D) an animal that eats only meat

NOTES

The Koala

Most people think of koalas as koala bears, but they are not bears. They are really marsupials and are in the same family as the wombat. Koalas live in a special place called a eucalyptus forest. They can be found in eastern and southeastern Australia. Adult koalas are one of only three animals that can live on a diet of eucalyptus leaves. These leaves contain 50% water so they rarely need to drink extra water.

The koala is a marsupial which means the baby crawls into a pocket, called a pouch, on the mother's tummy as soon as it is born. Baby koalas are called "joeys." When they are born, they cannot see, have no hair, and are less than one inch long. They stay in their mother's pouch for the next six months. First their mother feeds them her milk. Then she feeds them a food called "pap" in addition to her milk. Joeys continue to take their mother's milk until they are a year old. The young koala will remain with its mother until another joey is born and comes into the pouch.

Question Number: 1   RI.4.1

What detail in the text explains why someone is not likely to see a koala in northwestern Australia?

Ⓐ   Koalas live in a special place called a eucalyptus forest.
Ⓑ   They are really marsupials and are in the same family as the wombat.
Ⓒ   Koalas live...in eastern and south-eastern Australia.
Ⓓ   When they are born, they are blind, hairless, and less than one inch long.

Question Number: 2   RI.4.7

Which picture or illustration would not help the reader understand the above text and should not be included?

Ⓐ   a picture of an adult koala
Ⓑ   a picture of a newborn 'joey'
Ⓒ   a picture of a polar bear
Ⓓ   a map showing areas where koalas are found naturally

The Different Tissues of the Human Body

There are four types of tissues that are created as cells join together and work as a group. Each type of tissue has a unique structure and does a specific job. Muscle tissue is made up of long, narrow muscle cells. Muscle tissue makes your body parts move by tightening and relaxing. Connective tissue is what holds up your body and connects its parts together. Bone is made up of connective tissue. Nerve tissue is made up of long nerve cells that go through your body and carry messages. Epithelial tissue is made of wide, flat epithelial cells. This tissue lines the surfaces inside the body and forms the outer layer of the skin. Groups of tissue join together to form the organs in our body such as the heart, liver, lungs, brain, and kidneys just to name a few. Then these organs work together to form our body systems. Each system works together, and with the other systems of the body.

Muscle Tissue	Connective Tissue	Nerve Tissue	Epithelial Tissue
- long, narrow cells - contracts and relaxes causing movement	- holds up the body - connects body parts together	- long cells - carries messages throughout the body	- wide, flat cells - lines inside surfaces - forms outer skin layer

Question Number: 1   RI.4.1

What job does muscle tissue perform in the body?

Ⓐ It holds up your body.
Ⓑ It allows your body to move
Ⓒ It allows messages to travel through your body.
Ⓓ It forms the outer layer of skin.

Question Number: 2   RI.4.1

What job does the epithelial tissue perform?

Ⓐ It holds up your body.
Ⓑ It allows your body to move.
Ⓒ It allows messages to travel through your body.
Ⓓ It forms the outer layer of skin.

Question Number: 3   RI.4.7

How does the chart help the reader understand the functions of each of the four types of tissues?

Ⓐ It adds details not mentioned in the text so the reader can gather more information.
Ⓑ It elaborates on details mentioned in the text.
Ⓒ It changes some of the details mentioned in the text.
Ⓓ It clarifies the details mentioned in the text by categorizing them by tissue type.

Question Number: 4   RI.4.7

Which types of tissue have similarly shaped cells?

Ⓐ Epithelial tissue and connective tissue
Ⓑ Muscle tissue and connective tissue
Ⓒ Connective tissue and nerve tissue
Ⓓ Muscle tissue and nerve tissue

Question Number: 5   RI.4.7

To help the reader visualize what each tissue looks like, what would be the BEST visual aid to include with this text?

Ⓐ A drawing of the heart, liver, lungs, brain, and kidneys
Ⓑ Microscopic views of each type of tissue
Ⓒ A diagram of a nerve cell
Ⓓ A chart providing information about each type of tissue

48

The Toy Story

2362 West Main Street
Jojo, TX 98456

June 16, 2010

Dear Mr. Seymour:

I ordered a Magic Racing Top from your company. The toy was delivered to me today in a package that was badly damaged. I took a picture of the box before I opened it, which I am sending to you as proof of damage. The toy inside was broken due, I'm sure, to the damage to the package during shipping.

This toy was to be a gift for my friend's birthday. There is not enough time before his party to wait on a replacement toy; therefore, I no longer need the toy. I would like for you to refund my money. If you would like for me to return the broken toy, please send a prepaid shipping label. Thank you for handling this matter for me. I look forward to hearing from you and hope we can satisfactorily resolve this problem.

Sincerely,
Tim West

Question Number: 1   **RI.4.1**

Dominique argues that the writer of this letter was pleased with the toy company because he says, "please," and "if you would like." Does this evidence do a good job of supporting her argument?

Ⓐ Yes. These are very polite words, so he is clearly pleased with the toy company.
Ⓑ Yes. He also says, "Thank you for handling this matter for me."
Ⓒ No. He is being polite, but he also says the package he ordered was, "badly damaged," and, "I would like for you to refund my money."
Ⓓ No. He wants to satisfactorily resolve the problem.

Question Number: 2   RI.4.8

What evidence does the writer of this letter offer to support his claim that the package arrived damaged?

Ⓐ The toy was broken.
Ⓑ He wanted a replacement or a refund.
Ⓒ He is sending a picture of the damaged package.
Ⓓ He wants to satisfactorily resolve the problem.

Question Number: 3   RI.4.8

The author does not want a replacement toy. What reason does he give for not wanting a replacement?

Ⓐ The package was damaged during shipping.
Ⓑ The toy was a gift, and there is not enough time to ship a replacement.
Ⓒ The toy is broken.
Ⓓ He requests a prepaid shipping label to return the toy.

Shells Saga

Beautiful seashells that are washed ashore on beaches by ocean waves have always amazed people. Shells come in a wonderful collection of shapes, sizes, and colors. Shells are actually made by marine creatures to serve as their homes. Seashells are, quite simply, skeletons of mollusks. Mollusks are a class of water animals that have soft bodies and hard outer coverings, called shells. People carry their bony skeletons inside and wear their soft bodies on the outside. But mollusks do just the opposite. Shells protect the soft-bodied animals from rough surfaces that can harm their bodies and from predators.

Shells are very <u>durable</u> and last longer than the soft-bodied animals that make and wear them. Shells may be univalve or bivalve. Univalve shells are made up of just one unit. Bivalve shells have two units or two halves. Snails have univalve shells and oysters have bivalve shells.

Question Number: 1   RI.4.2

The main role of a seashell is:

Ⓐ to look beautiful
Ⓑ to serve as a home for mollusks
Ⓒ to float to the shores
Ⓓ to be collected by divers

Question Number: 2   RI.4.4

What is the meaning of the underlined word ?

Ⓐ Soft-bodied
Ⓑ Outlive
Ⓒ Protect
Ⓓ Tough

Sacagawea

Sacagawea is a famous Native American from the Shoshone tribe. She became famous when she helped two men, explorers named Lewis and Clark, find their way through the unknown west. When she was 12 years old, she was kidnapped by an enemy Native American tribe called the Hidatsa. Then, legend has it, the chief of the Hidatsa tribe sold Sacagawea into slavery.

In 1804, she became a translator and guide for a group of explorers led by Lewis and Clark. She helped them find their way from near the Dakotas to the Pacific Ocean. She became a famous Native American in our history for being brave and helping these men discover unknown territory.

Question Number: 1   RI.4.2

What would be a good title for the above story?

Ⓐ Sacagawea: A Shoshone Woman
Ⓑ Sacagawea: An Amazing Woman
Ⓒ Sacagawea: Kidnapped by the Hidatsa
Ⓓ Sacagawea: Sold to a Fur Trader

Question Number: 2   RI.4.2

What is the main idea of the story above?

Ⓐ Sacagawea's life was amazing.
Ⓑ Sacagawea was a woman who did so many things that women didn't do at the time.
Ⓒ Sacagawea helped two men explore the west.
Ⓓ What Sacagawea did will be remembered forever.

Question Number: 3   RI.4.5

How is the text written?

Ⓐ Compare and Contrast
Ⓑ Cause and Effect
Ⓒ Chronological
Ⓓ Problem and Solution

Question Number: 4

How could this passage be rewritten so it becomes a comparative essay?   **RI.4.5**

Ⓐ Dates could be added to the passage.
Ⓑ Excerpts from Sacagawea's personal diary could be added.
Ⓒ Directions and maps from the journey could be added.
Ⓓ Quotations could be added to the passage.

Question Number: 5

Which of the pictures below best represents what is being explained in the text?
RI.4.7

Ⓐ

Ⓑ

Ⓒ

Ⓓ None of the above

Bichon Frise

Bichon frise is a very different breed of dog. They have white fluffy hair and tiny, black eyes. Years ago, this funny little breed was used as circus dogs. Many people keep them as pets, because they are hypoallergenic. This means that people with allergies aren't allergic to them. They don't shed, so they won't leave hair all over your house.

Question Number: 1   RI.4.2

What is the main idea of the passage?

- Ⓐ Bichon frise is a unique breed of dogs.
- Ⓑ Bichon frise used to be circus dogs.
- Ⓒ Bichon frise are hypoallergenic.
- Ⓓ Bichon frise have white hair and black eyes.

Question Number: 2   RI.4.5

What is the text structure of the above passage?

- Ⓐ Cause and Effect
- Ⓑ Compare and contrast
- Ⓒ Problem and Solution
- Ⓓ Narrative

Digestive System

The digestive system is made up of the esophagus, stomach, liver, gall bladder, pancreas, large and small intestines, appendix, and rectum. Digestion actually begins in the mouth when food is chewed and mixed with saliva. Muscles in the esophagus push food into the stomach. Once there, it mixes with digestive juices. While in the stomach, food is broken down into nutrients, things good for you, and turned into a thick liquid. The food then moves into the small intestines where more digestive juices complete breaking it down. It is in the small intestines that nutrients are taken into the blood and carried throughout the body. Anything left over that your body cannot use goes to the large intestine. The body takes water from those leftovers. The rest is passed out of your body.

Question Number: 1   RI.4.3

What event begins the digestive process?

Ⓐ The small intestine absorbing nutrients
Ⓑ Muscles in the esophagus pushing food into the stomach
Ⓒ Chewing food and allowing it to mix with saliva
Ⓓ The esophagus

Question Number: 2   RI.4.3

How do nutrients that are absorbed from food move though the body?

Ⓐ They develop the ability to swim through the body's fluids in a tiny school bus.
Ⓑ The digestive juices in the small intestine break them down.
Ⓒ They move through the esophagus and into the stomach.
Ⓓ They are absorbed into the blood, which carries them to other parts of the body.

Question Number: 3   RI.4.7

What visual aid should be included with the above text to enhance student understanding?

Ⓐ a diagram of the digestive system
Ⓑ a diagram of the mouth
Ⓒ a diagram of food
Ⓓ a diagram of stomach tissue

Question Number: 4   **RI.4.8**

What evidence does the writer provide to support the fact that everything eaten is not used by the body for nutrients?

(A) Digestion actually begins in the mouth when food is chewed and mixed with saliva.

(B) The food then moves into the small intestines where more digestive juices complete breaking it down.

(C) It is in the small intestines that nutrients are taken into the blood and carried throughout the body.

(D) Anything left over that your body cannot use goes to the large intestine. The body takes water from those leftovers. The rest is passed out of your body.

Matter

All matter, which makes up all things, can be changed in two ways: chemically and physically. Both chemical and physical changes affect the state of matter. Physical changes are those that do not change what the matter is made of. For example, clay will flatten if squeezed, but it will still be clay. Changing the shape of clay is a physical change and does not change the matter's identity. Chemical changes turn the matter into a something new. For example, when paper is burned, it becomes ash and will never be paper again. The difference between them is that physical changes are temporary or only last for a little while. Chemical changes are permanent, which means they last forever. Physical and chemical changes both affect the state of matter.

Question Number: 1   RI.4.3

Which sentence below explains the concept of physical change?

(A) Physical change occurs when matter goes through a a change that makes something new.
(B) Physical change occurs when a person gains or loses weight.
(C) Physical change is change that occurs naturally and affects the state of matter.
(D) Physical change is change that does not make something new.

Question Number: 2   RI.4.3

Which sentence below explains the concept of chemical change?

(A) Chemical change is change that does not make something new.
(B) Chemical changes occur when something new is made
(C) Chemical change occurs when someone mixes unknown chemicals in a beaker.
(D) Chemical change occurs when clay is flattened or squeezed.

Question Number: 3   RI.4.3

What is the primary difference between physical and chemical change?

(A) Physical changes affect the state of matter, while chemical changes do not.
(B) Chemical changes are temporary, while chemical changes are permanent.
(C) Physical changes are temporary, while chemical changes are permanent.
(D) Chemical and physical changes make something entirely new.

Question Number: 4   **RI.4.5**

What type of structure did they use to write this paragraph?

Ⓐ Compare and Contrast
Ⓑ Cause and Effect
Ⓒ Chronological
Ⓓ Problem and Solution

Lewis and Clark Enlist Help

Sacagawea, also spelled Sacajawea, is best known for her role in helping Meriwether Lewis and William Clark during their journey to explore the American West. They set out on their journey on May 14, 1804. They left from near what is now Wood River, Illinois; but it was that winter in South Dakota when they met Sacagawea. They reached the Pacific Ocean on the coast of Oregon in November 1805.

A journey like this had never been done before. Now, we call this land the American West. In those days it was a new frontier full of unknown native people and dangerous land. Without the help of someone who knew the land, Lewis and Clark may not have made it to the Pacific.

Sacagawea was the young Shoshone wife of a French-Canadian fur trapper named Toussaint Charbonneau. Together, she and her husband served as interpreters, guides, and negotiators for Lewis and Clark. Their friendship with Clark was so strong that when they returned, they moved to his hometown of St. Louis. Clark even became the guardian of her children after her death.

Question Number: 1   **RI.4.3**

Which of the following sentences best explains how important Sacagawea was to Lewis and Clark's expedition?

Ⓐ Sacagawea was a member of the Shoshone tribe of Native Americans.
Ⓑ Because they were travelling unknown territory, they needed the help of a person who knew about the people they would encounter and the land they would navigate.
Ⓒ Sacagawea could not have aided the Lewis and Clark expedition without the help of her husband, who was an experienced fur trapper.
Ⓓ Because Sacagawea was Shoshone by birth and married to a French-Canadian man, she spoke two languages.

Theories behind extinction of the Dinosaurs

There are many theories about how dinosaurs came to be extinct. Scientists do not all agree about what may have happened. The most recent idea says that a giant meteorite crashed into the earth. It kicked up enough dust and dirt that the Sun's rays did not reach Earth for a very long time. This prevented plants from making their own food via photosynthesis. In turn, plant-eaters died for lack of food. After that, meat-eaters followed.

The other leading idea says that dinosaurs died out when the Earth went through a time when volcanoes were erupting. Like the meteorite idea, it is thought that the volcanoes spewed enough ash into the air that the Sun's rays were blocked. This also caused plant and animal life to die.

Question Number: 1   RI.4.3

According to the passage, How can lack of sunlight cause animals to become extinct?

Ⓐ   It disrupts the food chain starting with producers. If plants die out, then plant-eaters have nothing to eat. If plant-eaters starve and die out, then meat-eaters have nothing to eat and also die.

Ⓑ   Dinosaurs became extinct because of widespread volcanic eruptions that blocked sunlight from reaching Earth. When this happened, plants died, beginning a disruption of the food chain that dinosaurs didn't survive.

Ⓒ   One theory suggests a meteorite caused dinosaur extinction, while another claims widespread volcanic eruptions caused the animals to die. Both theories, however, center around the idea that plants did not get needed sunlight and plant-eating and meat-eating animals died as a result.

Ⓓ   It creates a shadow over the entire planet which makes everything very cold. This extreme cold keeps the animals from being able to hunt or eat.

Question Number: 2   RI.4.3

Do all scientests agree about how dinosaurs became extinct?

Ⓐ   No. The text explains that there are many theories on dinosaur extinction and describes two of them.
Ⓑ   No. Some scientists believe dinosaurs died when a giant meteorite crashed into earth, while others blame extraterrestrials.
Ⓒ   Yes. The scientific community has debated several possibilities, and they agree that dinosaurs died out as the result of widespread volcanic eruptions.
Ⓓ   Yes. The scientists have argued but finally agree that they dinosaurs became extinct when a meteor crashed into Earth.

Childhood Obesity

In the United States today, we are starting to see more and more of a problem with children who are overweight. Doctors and even the President's wife are trying to do something about it. They are recommending healthier foods and that children get daily vigorous exercise. They also recommend that children go outside and do things instead of sitting in front of the tv. They have suggested that children get at least an hour of exercise a day by doing things like jumping rope or cycling, or anything else that makes their hearts beat faster. This kind of exercise is known as aerobic exercise. Something else they recommend is for children to do exercises that strengthen the bones and muscles. There are lots of ways children can do this. One way is running.

Question Number: 1   RI.4.4

What is the meaning of vigorous in the above text?

Ⓐ slow
Ⓑ growing well
Ⓒ energetic, forceful
Ⓓ weak

Question Number: 2   RI.4.8

What is the main idea of the above text?

Ⓐ Doctors want you to move.
Ⓑ It is very important for kids to exercise daily.
Ⓒ Jumping and other activities help make your bones strong.
Ⓓ Any physical exercise helps make your heart beat stronger.

NOTES

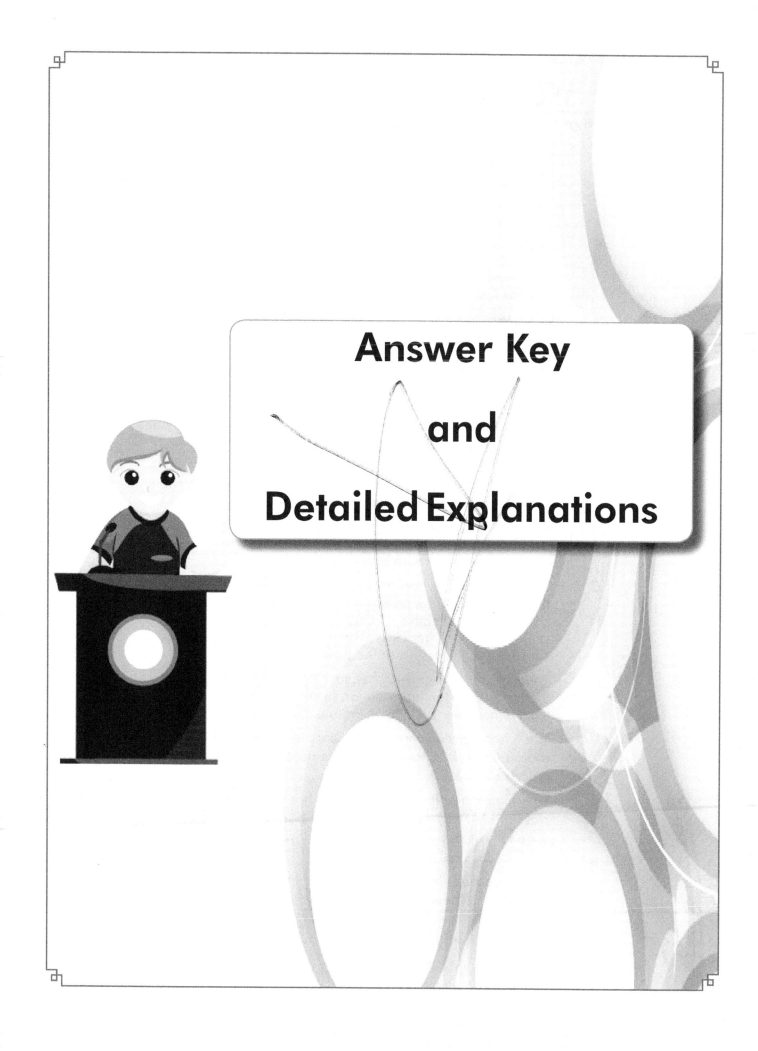

Answer Key

and

Detailed Explanations

The Elephant Who Saw the World

Question No.	Answer	Detailed Explanations	CCSS
1	B	The second choice is correct. When Mary began reading her story to her class, those are the first words she read. The title of a story goes at the top of the page, and those are the first words read when sharing a story aloud.	RL.4.1
2	C	The third choice is correct. The passage states that "However, there was one part about every Friday at school that Mary did not enjoy, and that was when she had to share her story in front of the class."	RL.4.1
3	C	The third choice is correct, because the passage stated that, "The teacher made all the children share on Friday afternoons."	RL.4.1
4	B	The second choice is correct. We can infer that Mary began reading her story in front of the class, because the last sentence said that she got out of her seat and walked to the front of the room after her name was called. We know that was the signal to start reading the story.	RL.4.1
5	C	The third choice is correct. The passage tells us that Mary really enjoys writing stories. We know that many parents support their children at things they are good at.	RL.4.1
6	C	The third choice is correct, because it tells the most important details from the passage. The other options either give too little or too much information.	RL.4.2
7	C	The third choice is correct, because it has nothing to do with the main idea of the passage. The passage is about Mary being good at creative writing, but being afraid to share her stories in front of her class. The third choice is correct, because it wasn't even from the passage.	RL.4.2
8	A	The first choice is correct, because it tells the main idea and the most important information from the story. The other options either give too little or too much information.	RL.4.2
9	C	The third choice is correct. The story takes place in her classroom at Mary's school. The whole passage is about one of Mary's classes.	RL.4.3
10	C	The third choice is correct. Sharing her story in front of the class made Mary nervous. The third paragraph in the passage tells us this.	RL.4.3
11	B	The picture of the female in front of a chalkboard is appropriate, because this story takes place in a school classroom and Mary is speaking to her class.	RL.4.7

Alex the Great

Question No.	Answer	Detailed Explanations	CCSS
1	D	According to the story, Alexander realized "that the horse was terrified of its own shadow, and he turned the horse towards the sun so that its shadow fell behind it. This calmed the horse, and the prince proudly rode away."	RL.4.1
2	C	The third choice is correct. We know the horse was scared, because the passage said "Realizing that the horse was terrified of its own shadow." Terrified means the same thing as scared.	RL.4.1
3	A	The first choice is correct. The first sentence of the passage tells us that the story takes place two thousand five hundred years ago.	RL.4.3
4	B	The second choice is correct, because the entire passage was how Alexander figured out how to tame the horse (smartness) and how he became a great man in history (greatness).	RL.4.2

My Vacation in Hawaii

1	D	The fourth choice is correct. It referred to the vacation as a "nightmare," and told that they "cut their trip short." If they were enjoying their trip, they would have stayed the whole time as planned instead of leaving early.	RL.4.1
2	A	The first answer choice is correct. Because the author wished the vacation could have been two weeks instead of one shows that the vacation was wonderful.	RL.4.1
3	B	Their favorite vacation spot was Hawaii and option B describes the hotel in Hawaii. Options C and D are statements that describe the Hawaii vacation but they do not describe the hotel.	RL.4.1
4	B	This is a compare and contrast passage, because it tells the similarities and differences of two different subjects.	RL.4.5
5	C	Problem and solution texts describe a problem, then they explain a solution to the problem. Germs are a problem, and the passage explains how to deal with them.	RL.4.5
6	C	The third choice is correct, because it tells how the people favored the Hawaiian vacation over the Alaskan vacation.	RL.4.9

The Surprise Vacation

Question No.	Answer	Detailed Explanations	CCSS
1	A	The first choice is correct. We can infer that it is summer, because the passage tells us that it is hot. We know that people go surfing in the summertime because the hot weather makes the ocean just right for swimming and surfing.	RL.4.1
2	B	The second choice is correct. We can infer that Susie's family lives near the beach, because the passage says that they drove there in a car. If they did not live near the beach, they would have to travel for several hours or fly on an airplane to get to the beach. The passage did not imply that they would be traveling a long distance.	RL.4.1
3	C	Sequencing and Chronological texts tell about events in the order that they happened.	RL.4.5

Fred Goes to the Dentist

1	C	The third choice is correct. Fred spent a lot of time worrying about visiting the dentist and got himself really worked up. When he actually visited the dentist, nothing bad happened to him. He realized that he was wrong for worrying.	RL.4.2
2	B	The second choice is correct. We know that Fred was afraid and didn't understand why he had to go to the dentist, because the passage said that he had heard horror stories all of his life about the dentist and he thought the dentist would torture him. The passage also said that he didn't understand why his mom thought he needed to go since none of his teeth were hurting.	RL.4.3
3	C	The third choice is correct. We know that Fred felt relieved after his visit to the dentist, because he said the chair was comfortable and the dentist was nice. The last sentence of the passage said that it wasn't as bad as he thought it would be.	RL.4.3
4	B	The second choice is correct. The setting for the second paragraph is an automobile, because it tells us that Fred and his mother were on their way to the dentist. People usually take automobiles to the dentist.	RL.4.3
5	C	The third choice is correct. We know that Fred is worried about going to the dentist because people who are scared often tremble in fear.	RL.4.3

Question No.	Answer	Detailed Explanations	CCSS
6	B	The second choice is correct. We know that Fred thinks the dentist will put him in a chair and use a huge drill on him, because that is what the second paragraph of the passage is about.	RL.4.3
7	A	The first choice is correct. The last paragraph of the passage tells us that the dentist showed Fred how to brush and floss his teeth.	RL.4.3
8	C	The third choice is correct, because it most accurately describes how Fred was afraid at first and then relieved after he saw the dentist.	RL.4.9

Honesty is the Best Policy

1	B	The second choice is correct. Opal felt really bad when she acted dishonestly. After she told the truth, she instantly felt better.	RL.4.2
2	B	The second choice is correct, because it tells the most important information in the passage. The other options either give too little or too much information.	RL.4.2
3	C	Third person point of view is when the story is told by someone who is not a character in the story.	RL.4.6

The Christmas Gift

1	A	The first choice is correct. The quilt did not cost much money, but it had a lot of sentimental value to Libby.	RL.4.2
2	B	The second choice is correct. In this story, a homemade gift (the quilt) was better than an expensive one, but that is a detail and not the theme.	RL.4.2
3	A	The first choice is correct. Libby's grandmother was nervous, because she was afraid that Libby would not like the quilt.	RL.4.3
4	D	The fourth choice is correct. Libby's grandmother was happy after Libby opened up the quilt, because Libby loved the present.	RL.4.3

The Dental Nightmare

Question No.	Answer	Detailed Explanations	CCSS
1	A	The first choice is correct, because it tells only the most important information from the passage. Options B and C do not give enough information and Option D basically retells the entire story instead of just summarizing it.	RL.4.2
2	A	First person point of view is when one of the characters is telling the story. Pronouns such as I and me are used.	RL.4.6

Huckleberry Hound

1	A	The first choice is correct, because it gives only the most important information from the passage. Some of the information in the other answer choices is out of order. Options B and D also do not summarize because they leave in too much information.	RL.4.2
2	C	Third person point of view is when the story is told by someone who is not a character in the story.	RL.4.6

Oops! My Icecream!

1	A	The first choice is correct, because it tells the most important information in the passage. Option B is correct but does not include all of the key information. Options C and D do not summarize the paragraph.	RL.4.2
2	B	The second choice is correct. The writer was at school. The second sentence of the passage tells us so.	RL.4.3
3	A	The first choice is correct. The writer dropped her ice cream at the ice cream shop. The last sentence of the passage tells us so.	RL.4.3
4	A	First person point of view is when one of the characters in the story is telling it. Pronouns such as I and me are used.	RL.4.6

Bee Attack

Question No.	Answer	Detailed Explanations	CCSS
1	C	The third choice is correct, because it gives the main idea of the passage and the most important details. The other options either give too little or too much information.	RL.4.2
2	A	The first choice is correct. The first choice is not an important piece of information from the story. The other options are necessary for the summary.	RL.4.2
3	B	The second choice is correct. The story takes place outside in a yard. The first sentence of the passage tells us so.	RL.4.3

Timothy

1	C	The third choice is correct. We know that Timothy is responsible, because the passage said that he gets up early every day to perform his dog walking job. We know that Timothy is ambitious, because Timothy believes he can continue his dog walking job and participate in extracurricular activities at the same time.	RL.4.3
2	B	The second answer is correct. We know that Timothy wouldn't help someone cheat on a test, because the passage said that "he is always honest and expects others to be honest."	RL.4.3
3	C	The third choice is correct. We know Timothy is saving up for youth camp, because the last sentence of the passage tells us so.	RL.4.3
4	B	The second choice is correct. We know that Timothy gets up at 5 a.m. to walk dogs, because the third sentence of the second paragraph tells us so.	RL.4.3

The Two Brothers

Question No.	Answer	Detailed Explanations	CCSS
1	A	The first choice is correct. Stanley is solitary, because he likes to spend his time doing things by himself. Stanley is caring, because he volunteers at the recycling center.	RL.4.3
2	A	The first choice is correct. We know that Adam and Stanley like and respect each other, because they enjoy volunteering together at the recycling center.	RL.4.3
3	B	The second choice is correct. We know that Adam is thoughtful, because he volunteers his time at a recycling center. We know that Adam is outgoing, because he likes to spend all of his time with his friends.	RL.4.3
4	D	The fourth choice is correct. The last paragraph of the passage tells us that Adam and Stanley enjoy volunteering at the youth center together.	RL.4.3

Weekend Vacation

1	C	The third choice is correct. The third paragraph says "at the end of the school day."	RL.4.3
2	D	The fourth choice is correct. The kids were excited about being dismissed from school, and Aunt Margaret happened to be in the way. A scuff is only a very small mark.	RL.4.3
3	C	The third choice is correct. The parents are going out of town. The first sentence of the passage tells us this.	RL.4.3
4	D	This is a narrative text, because the writer is describing an event in his or her life.	RL.4.5

Shopping Frenzy

1	D	Sequencing and Chronological Order texts tell the events in the order that they happened.	RL.4.5
2	C	Third person point of view is when the story is being told by a person who is not a character in the story.	RL.4.6

Water, Water Everywhere but not a Drop to Drink!

Question No.	Answer	Detailed Explanations	CCSS
1	C	The third choice is correct, because it correctly tells where they used to get their water.	RL.4.9
2	D	Murky in color means dark, dingy, and cloudy. The water was very dirty and dark.	RI.4.4

The Ostrich

1	D	The fourth answer choice is correct. The author says the ostrich, "cannot fly," and that, "it can travel faster by running." Traveling faster is an advantage for the ostrich.	RI.4.1
2	D	The fourth answer choice is correct. By saying, "one of their favorite companions," the author implies the ostrich has many companions. The ostrich is not shy and solitary if it has many companions.	RI.4.1
3	B	Option B is the correct main idea. Although each of the other options can be found in the passage they are simply details and are not the main idea.	RI.4.2
4	A	The correct answer is A. Options B and C are incorrect statements and although option D is a correct statement, it does not support the main idea.	RI.4.2

The Blue Whale

Question No.	Answer	Detailed Explanations	CCSS
1	A	"Solitary" means alone. The first answer choice is correct because the statement contrasts the blue whale's behavior with the behavior of other whales that live in pods.	RI.4.1
2	C	The third choice is correct. The text says, "they surface to breathe air into their lungs through blowholes. They emerge from the ocean, spewing water out of their blowhole, roll, and reenter the water with a grand splash of their large tail." Choice A is false, while choice B has the order of events incorrect.	RI.4.3
3	A	The first choice is correct. The text says, "They make loud, deep, and rumbling low frequency sounds that travel great distances, which allow them to communicate with other whales as far as 100 miles away."	RI.4.3
4	B	Resonating means loud, because the passage says that their resonating sound makes them the loudest animal on earth.	RI.4.4
5	D	Descriptive text structures give characteristics of a particular topic in no particular order.	RI.4.5
6	B	Compare/contrast passages tell how subjects are alike and different.	RI.4.5
7	C	A picture of an adult blue whale would be helpful, because the passage describes what they look like and how large they are.	RI.4.7
8	C	The third choice is correct. It gives specific details about the size and weight of the blue whale's body.	RI.4.8
9	C	The third choice tells specifically how the whales communicate.	RI.4.8

The End of the Dinosaurs

Question No.	Answer	Detailed Explanations	CCSS
1	A	The first choice is correct. While the text does make a convincing case for the theory that a meteorite crashed into the Earth, causing dinosaurs to die out, the author implies that there are other theories by saying, "One such idea"	RI.4.1
2	C	Option C is the correct answer. Although each statement comes directly from the passage, only option C supports the main idea. As the sun was blocked from the dust, it killed off all plant life, leaving nothing for the dinosaurs to survive on.	RI.4.2
3	B	An herbivore is an animal that eats only plants. The passage gives us a clue when it said that the plants dying caused the herbivores to die.	RI.4.4
4	D	Carnivores are animals that eat only meat.	RI.4.4

The Koala

Question No.	Answer	Detailed Explanations	CCSS
1	C	The third answer choice is correct. The author does not include northwestern Australia as one of the areas koalas call home.	RI.4.1
2	C	A picture of a polar bear would not be helpful, because this passage is about koalas. Koalas are not bears.	RI.4.7

The Different Tissues of the Human Body

Question No.	Answer	Detailed Explanations	CCSS
1	B	The author writes that, "muscle tissue makes your body parts move by tightening and relaxing."	RI.4.1
2	D	The passage directly states epithelial tissue forms the outer layer of the skin.	RI.4.1
3	D	The fourth answer choice is correct. The chart makes the details clear by categorizing them according to tissue type. It does not add information or elaborate, but rather makes the information more concise. It does not change details.	RI.4.7
4	D	The fourth answer choice is correct. The chart makes it easy to see that both muscle tissue and nerve tissue have long cells.	RI.4.7
5	B	Microscopic views of each tissue type would show the reader exactly what each type looks like and how they are different.	RI.4.7

The Toy Story

1	C	The third choice is correct. Although the letter is polite, Tim West was displeased with his experience. Only dissatisfied customers ask for refunds.	RI.4.1
2	C	The third choice is correct. The picture is evidence that it was broken.	RI.4.8
3	B	The second choice is correct. In the letter, the boy states that there is not enough time before his friend's birthday for the company to send a replacement toy.	RI.4.8

Shells Saga

1	B	The second choice is correct, because the passage states that shells are made by marine creatures to serve as their homes.	RI.4.2
2	D	Durable means hardy and tough. The fact that shells often outlive the animals inside explains how tough they are.	RI.4.4

Sacagawea

Question No.	Answer	Detailed Explanations	CCSS
1	B	The second choice is correct, because the passage was about Sacagawea and the amazing things she did. Though the other titles are accurate, they only refer to parts of her story.	RI.4.2
2	A	The first choice is correct because it includes what the passage was about and the most important information. Although B is a correct statement, it is not covered in the passage.	RI.4.2
3	C	The text structure is chronological, because it gives the events in the order that they occurred.	RI.4.5
4	B	Adding passages from Sacagawea's personal diary would add a different perspective to the passage, allowing readers to view the information from two points of view and compare both sets of information.	RI.4.5
5	A	The picture of a Native American female is appropriate since the passage is about Sacagawea.	RI.4.7

Bichon Frise

1	A	The first choice is correct, because the whole passage is about how that type of dog is unique.	RI.4.2
2	D	The text structure is a narrative text because the writer is describing this dog breed.	RI.4.5

Digestive System

1	C	The third answer choice is correct. The text says, "Digestion actually begins in the mouth when food is chewed and mixed with saliva."	RI.4.3
2	D	The fourth choice is correct. The text says, "nutrients are absorbed into the blood and carried throughout the body."	RI.4.3
3	A	A diagram of the digestive system would be helpful so the reader could see what the different organs look like and where they are located compared to one another.	RI.4.7
4	D	The fourth choice tells what happens to the unabsorbed nutrients.	RI.4.8

Matter

Question No.	Answer	Detailed Explanations	CCSS
1	D	The fourth choice is correct. It explains the basic idea of physical change as described in the text.	RI.4.3
2	B	The second choice is correct. It explains the basic idea of chemical change as described in the text.	RI.4.3
3	C	The third choice is correct. The text says, "The difference between them is that physical changes are temporary or only last for a little while, and chemical changes are permanent, which means they last forever."	RI.4.3
4	A	The structure is compare/contrast, because it tells how chemical and physical changes are different.	RI.4.5

Lewis and Clark Enlist Help

Question No.	Answer	Detailed Explanations	CCSS
1	B	Because they were traveling unknown territory, they needed the help of a person who knew about the people they would encounter and the land they would navigate.	RI.4.3

Theories Behind Extinction of the Dinosaurs

Question No.	Answer	Detailed Explanations	CCSS
1	A	The first choice is correct. The text says, "..the Sun's rays did not reach Earth for a very long time, preventing plants from producing their own food via photosynthesis. In turn, plant-eaters died for lack of food, and then meat-eaters followed."	RI.4.3
2	A	The first choice is correct. The text says, "There are many theories about how dinosaurs came to be extinct." Then it goes on to describe two such theories: a meteorite collision and widespread volcanic eruptions.	RI.4.3

Childhood Obesity

Question No.	Answer	Detailed Explanations	CCSS
1	C	Vigorous means energetic and forceful. Exercise would be pointless if it wasn't energetic.	RI.4.4
2	B	The main idea is for kids to exercise. The entire passage is about this.	RI.4.8

Additional Practice Questions

Ellie the Ostrich has been extremely frustrated lately. Her friends Bailey and Jose run and play with her, but when they play tag she always loses! They start running and before she knows it, they are both fluttering around her head even though they are such small birds! It doesn't seem to matter that she is the largest bird in the world; she cannot fly. No matter how hard she flaps her wings, they just won't lift her off the ground. Her legs are so sturdy and extended that she can travel faster by running; but, Ellie doesn't want to run, she wants to fly and fly all across the sky.

One day, her father notices her friends flying away as a melancholy look flows over her face; he calls her to sit under the tree. "I know how hard it is to watch your smaller friends fly away, my sweet Ellie. But do you know how special your wings are?"

"No, Daddy." Ellie's shakes her head back and forth causing her feathers to shake from side to side.

"You can use your wings to help gather speed and swiftness when you start to run. You can also use them as brakes when turning and stopping which lets you stop very fast! In fact, our ostrich cousins have been known to run at a rate of 60 miles an hour which is faster than horses can run and as fast as most people drive cars."

"I can outrun a car?" she asks incredulously.

Ellie's dad grins. "You certainly can!"

"Wow! I think the next time they suggest tag, I'm going to suggest a race instead!"

Question Number: 1   RL.4.1

What is a detail that supports why Ellie travels faster by running?

Ⓐ Her legs are so strong and long that she can travel faster by running.
Ⓑ She can also use them as brakes in turning and stopping.
Ⓒ No matter how hard she flaps her wings, they just won't lift her off the ground.
Ⓓ Ellie doesn't want to run, she wants to fly and fly.

Question Number: 2   RL.4.1

According to Ellie's father, how do ostriches use their wings?

Ⓐ to help them to fly
Ⓑ as brakes while running
Ⓒ by flapping them
Ⓓ to keep them warm

One day, Ellie the Ostrich watched as two men entered her Aunt and Uncle's home. Moments later, they came out with handfuls of eggs. "Mama! Mama!" Ellie cried, running into her own house and flapping her wings to get her mother's attention.

"What is it, my sweet girl?"

"The eggs, Mama! They're stealing the eggs!" Tugging her mother's wings she pulled her out of the house and into the yard, watching with unhappy eyes as the men placed the eggs in distinct crates and drove off.

"Oh, honey, they're not stealing them." Ellie's mama explained. "These are eggs that will not become babies. Ostrich eggs are very special and the humans love to use them for food. They also make jewelry and cups with the egg shells."

Ellie's eyes got wider and wider as her mother continued talking. "They like our eggs that much and they weren't stealing them?"

Ellie's eyes got wider and wider as her mother continued talking. "Wow. They like our eggs that much and they weren't stealing them?"

"They do, Ellie and no, your Aunt and Uncle knew they were coming today. The men had an appointment; but, you did a wonderful job letting us know."

"I did?"

Spreading a large wing, Ellie's mother pulled her in for a hug. "Of course you did. Protecting our family is one of the most important jobs we will ever have and you did that beautifully!"

Question Number: 3   **RL.4.1**

Which detail describes the way ostrich eggs are used?

Ⓐ Ostriches have been known to run at the rate of 60 miles an hour.
Ⓑ Each Ostrich egg weighs one pound, which is as much as two dozen chicken eggs.
Ⓒ The shells also are made into cups and ornaments.
Ⓓ Ostrich eggs are delicious.

I found a shell, a curly one;
Lying on the sand.
I picked it up and took it home,
Held tightly in my hand.
Mommy looked at it and then,
She held it to my ear,
And from the shell there came a song
Soft and sweet and clear.
I was surprised, I listened hard,
And it was really true:
If you can find a nice big shell,
You'll hear the singing too.
--Unknown

Question Number: 4   RL.4.1

Why was the poet surprised?

Ⓐ She found a curly shell on the beach.
Ⓑ Her mother put it to her ear.
Ⓒ She didn't expect to hear a song from the shell.
Ⓓ She was frightened of the shell.

Cindy's mom called her to supper. When Cindy arrived in the kitchen, she looked at the food on the stove and made a face. She looked in the freezer and saw a frozen pizza and asked her mom if she could cook it instead.

Question Number: 5   RL.4.1

What can you infer from Cindy's actions?

Ⓐ That she was excited about what her mother had cooked
Ⓑ She was not very hungry for dinner.
Ⓒ She didn't think the meal was ready.
Ⓓ She didn't like what her mother cooked for dinner.

As Ben woke up on Sunday, he was thinking that it would be great to do something special with his dad that day, as he didn't see him very often. When he looked outside the window, he noticed that the sun was out but a new blanket of snow had fallen during the night. He was getting dressed thinking of what they could do when all of a sudden he heard his dad say, "It is a sunny day. Grab your skis on the way down!" Ben ran to get his skis and they left.

Question Number: 6   **RL.4.1**

Where do you think Ben and his dad were going?

Ⓐ to the zoo
Ⓑ to the mall
Ⓒ to the mountain
Ⓓ to school

Thelma lay on the windowsill. She heard a loud noise, so she lifted her head and looked outside. It woke her up and now she wasn't happy. The color of the sky was changing from dark to a light pinkish yellow and she could hear the birds starting to chirp. Her back arched high as she stretched a deep stretch. She figured it was time to go and find some food anyways because she was starting to get hungry.

Question Number: 7   **RL.4.1**

What time of day do you think this is happening?

Ⓐ in the evening at sunset
Ⓑ in the early afternoon
Ⓒ in the early morning at sunrise
Ⓓ in the middle of the day

Question Number: 8   **RL.4.1**

What kind of animal is Thelma?

Ⓐ a horse
Ⓑ a cricket
Ⓒ a mouse
Ⓓ a cat

Today was Rhonda's first day at her new school. She was very nervous and wished that she was going back to her old school; but, that was impossible since they had moved. Although she didn't have many friends at her old school, she would still prefer being back there because she knew the teachers, the routines, and the rules.

The first day, Rhonda met three girls that she really liked. They had all of their classes together so she spent much of the day with them. But Rhonda's favorite thing was that this school had art and music class; her old school had neither. Rhonda and her new friends had a great time in art that first day. She couldn't wait to go to music tomorrow. Maybe this new school wouldn't be so bad after all.

Question Number: 9   RL.4.2

What is the theme of the above passage?

Ⓐ Friends help each other.
Ⓑ Bullying hurts everyone.
Ⓒ Change can be good.
Ⓓ It's OK to be different.

Polly's little brother begged her to read him a story. She told him to go away, that she didn't have time to bother with him. But, a few minutes later, he came back and asked her again. This time she yelled at him to go away and she heard him crying as he ran down the hall. Later when she went to the family room, her mother told her that she had hurt her brother's feelings. Polly looked over at him and told him that she was sorry. Although she apologized, her little brother's feelings were still hurt; he felt like Polly didn't like to spend time with him. Polly's mom told her that sometimes words were not enough. So, when Polly got his favorite book and asked him to read with her, her little brother smiled and ran to sit by Polly. He hugged her and told her that she was the best big sister a boy could have.

Question Number: 10   RL.4.2

What can you learn from the above passage?

Ⓐ Knowledge is power.
Ⓑ Never give up.
Ⓒ Face your fears.
Ⓓ Actions speak louder than words.

Karen and Steve were both in Ms. Taylor's math class. Ms. Taylor wasn't very strict about when they had to turn their work in, and Steve took full advantage of that. He always did his homework for his other classes, but he would put off the work for Ms. Taylor's math assignments thinking he could do them later. However, Karen finished each assignment Ms. Taylor assigned right away. She had to work a little longer each night, but she didn't want to get marked down for turning in her math homework late. At the end of the semester, Karen and Steve both wanted to go to the amusement park. Ms. Taylor called Steve's mother to let her know about Steve not turning the work in on time, and she put Steve on restriction until all of his work was turned in. That was a horrible weekend for Steve. Even though he stayed up really late each night, he still couldn't finish everything. The whole time Steve was working, Karen had a great time eating hot dogs at the amusement park, watching movies, and having a great weekend.When they got their report cards, Steve was lucky to get by with a "C" minus in math while Karen got an "A."

Question Number: 11   RL.4.2

What did Karen and Steve learn from this?

Ⓐ It doesn't matter when you do it as long as it gets done.
Ⓑ Lazy people are sometimes rewarded with good things.
Ⓒ It's better to do things on time instead of putting them off for later.
Ⓓ Doing things early doesn't help you earn rewards in life.

Mr. Toad and Mr. Rabbit were eating at the food court of the shopping mall. Mr. Toad was eating many slices of pizza and drinking a huge soda, and Mr. Rabbit was watching him.

"Hey, Mr. Toad. If you give me some of your pizza, I'll let you have the next fly I find," called out Mr. Rabbit.

Mr. Toad said no, even though he was so full. "I'm sorry, Mr. Rabbit," Mr. Toad said, "but this pizza cost a lot so I can't share it."

Mr. Rabbit was sad and waited for Mr. Toad to finish. They then left the mall together. On their way out the door, a hunter saw them and started running after them. Mr. Toad normally could have escaped, but since he had eaten so much, Mr. Toad couldn't move another inch. The hunter caught him. Mr. Rabbit was able to escape easily.

Question Number: 12   RL.4.2

What is the theme of the story?

Ⓐ It's better to share.
Ⓑ If you paid for it, it's all yours.
Ⓒ Better late than never
Ⓓ Racing can be difficult.

84

Frank studied all the time, and he felt that he was very smart. One day at school, a student from Frank's class asked him if he wanted to go play baseball, but Frank said, "I've read all about baseball in books, and it sounds boring. No, thanks."

Another day, a different student asked Frank if he wanted to go and get hamburgers after school. Frank responded, "I've read that hamburgers are made with beef heart and organ meat. No, thank you."

Nobody wanted to ask Frank to go hang out again, but he did study about why it's important to have friends in his books.

Question Number: 13   RL.4.2

What would be an appropriate theme for the above passage?

Ⓐ It's not nice to be mean to your friends.
Ⓑ Friends are always getting in the way.
Ⓒ Learning from books is no substitute for real life experience.
Ⓓ Friendship gets in the way of learning important things.

A monkey put his hand into a jar of cookies and grasped as many as he could possibly hold. But, when he tried to pull out his hand it wouldn't fit! Unwilling to lose the cookies, and yet unable to pull out his hand, he burst into tears and cried about his situation.

Question Number: 14   RL.4.2

What would be an appropriate theme for the above passage?

Ⓐ The grass is always greener on the other side.
Ⓑ Always ask before taking.
Ⓒ Don't be greedy.
Ⓓ Work now and play later.

Mary walked quietly through the house so that she would not wake her parents. Before entering the kitchen, she stood and listened. She wanted to make sure that nobody had heard her and gotten up. She slowly opened the cabinet door, trying to make sure that it didn't squeak. As Mary reached into the cabinet, something warm and furry touched her hand. Mary ran from the kitchen screaming loudly. Her father ran in to see what had happened. He started laughing when he saw their cat Purr Purr sitting quietly in the kitchen cabinet wagging her tail.

Question Number: 15   **RL.4.2**

Choose the best summary of the above text.

Ⓐ Mary went to the kitchen. She stopped and listened. She opened the cabinet. She
      screamed. Her dad laughed.
Ⓑ Mary snuck quietly into the kitchen. When she opened the cabinet, something touched
      her hand and made her scream. Her dad came to help and discovered it was their
      cat in the cabinet.
Ⓒ The cat hid in the cabinet and scared Mary when she reached into it.
Ⓓ Mary walked into the kitchen after listening to make sure that nobody heard her. She
      opened the cabinet slowly and felt something touch her. She ran away screaming.
      She didn't know it was her cat Purr Purr.

It was the last round of the school spelling bee and only two students were left. Beau's heart was pounding and he was sweating. He began fidgeting with the button on one of his shirt sleeves.

Question Number: 16   **RL.4.3**

Which adjective describes how Beau was feeling?

Ⓐ anxious
Ⓑ proud
Ⓒ depressed
Ⓓ envious

Huckleberry Hound was sitting on the front porch. Suddenly he jumped to his feet and ran through the yard and into the field next to his house. When he got to the field, he put his nose to the ground and started sniffing as he walked. Yep, he definitely smelled a rabbit. He raised his head and howled loudly to let the other dogs know what he had found. Then, he shot after the rabbit like a bolt of lightning. He chased that rabbit for what seemed like hours around that field, but he never caught it. He returned to his yard with his head hanging and his tail tucked between his legs.

86

Question Number: 17   RL.4.3

At the beginning of the story, where was Huckleberry Hound?

Ⓐ   in the yard
Ⓑ   in a field
Ⓒ   on the porch
Ⓓ   in his kennel

Question Number: 18   RL.4.3

Where did Huckleberry Hound chase the rabbit?

Ⓐ   in the yard
Ⓑ   in a field
Ⓒ   on the porch
Ⓓ   in his kennel

Question Number: 19   RL.4.3

Where was Huckleberry Hound at the end of the story?

Ⓐ   in the yard
Ⓑ   in a field
Ⓒ   on the porch
Ⓓ   in his kennel

Read the two passages and answer the question that follow.

Passage 1

"The Elephant Who Saw the World," Mary started speaking. It was Friday, and the students had to share their creative writing stories of the week.

Mary loved writing, and this part of the week, when they were able to make up stories for creative writing, was her favorite part. She enjoyed it so much she became really good at it. When she was home on the weekends and she didn't have much homework, she would sit in her room for hours and create stories to share with her friends and family. Her parents always supported her and were her biggest fans.

However, there was one part about every Friday at school that Mary did not enjoy, and that was when she had to share her story in front of the class. The teacher made all of the children share on Friday afternoons, and this made Mary very nervous. She was shy, and although she knew her teacher was right, she didn't like it.

After sitting and listening to the other children share, Mary finally heard her name called. She knew it was her turn to share. She got out of her seat slowly, walked to the front of the room and began.

Passage 2

Timmy grabbed his paper and ran to the front of the classroom. Today was the day! He was so excited to finally have a chance to tell his story. He loved writing and his mind swam with ideas but he couldn't seem to get them all out. For weeks, he had worked and worked so hard to get the right words down on the page.

Finally, during writing time this week, his ideas gelled and the words flowed, creating the most exciting piece of work possible. His story was sure to capture the minds of his classmates and they would want him to tell stories again and again. He was even ready to read the story aloud, having practiced different voices for the different characters and parts of the story.

As he sat and listened to the other children, he bubbled over with excitement and anticipation. Hearing his name, he jumped up and ran to the front of the classroom. "Long ago," Timmy began, "a spaceship came and landed on my grandfather's barn..."

Question Number: 20   **RL.4.3**

Which choices below accurately describe Mary and Timmy's feelings about presenting to the class?

Ⓐ Mary loved writing; Timmy struggled to get the words right.
Ⓑ Timmy loved writing; Mary struggled to get the words right.
Ⓒ Mary was shy; Timmy was very excited.
Ⓓ Timmy was shy; Mary was very excited.

Question Number: 21   RL.4.4

Her eyes twinkled like diamonds as she looked lovingly at her new kitten.
Identify the simile used in the above sentence.

Ⓐ her eyes twinkled
Ⓑ as she looked lovingly
Ⓒ at her new kitten
Ⓓ twinkled like diamonds

Question Number: 22   RL.4.4

Elaine has no sympathy for others. You know she has a heart of stone.
Identify the metaphor in the above passage.

Ⓐ no sympathy for others
Ⓑ a heart of stone
Ⓒ no sympathy
Ⓓ she has a heart

Question Number: 23   RL.4.4

Identify the sentence that contains a metaphor.

Ⓐ She is as sweet as sugar.
Ⓑ She is as blind as a bat.
Ⓒ The sound of the chirping birds is music to my ears.
Ⓓ Billy is as stubborn as a mule.

Question Number: 24   RL.4.4

Suzy eats like a bird.
This simile means that Suzy:

Ⓐ eats nuts and seeds
Ⓑ eats many large meals
Ⓒ eats while flying
Ⓓ eats very little

Question Number: 25   RL.4.4

My wife is my compass that guides me to the correct paths in life.
The metaphor in the above passage compares his wife to:

Ⓐ a passage
Ⓑ compass
Ⓒ a guide
Ⓓ life

Question Number: 26   RL.4.4

I really got a bad deal on the used car I bought. That <u>car was a real lemon</u>.
The metaphor in this passage is used to let you know that the car:

Ⓐ was a good buy
Ⓑ had a very low price
Ⓒ was yellow
Ⓓ didn't run well

Question Number: 27   RL.4.4

Choose the answer that contains a simile.

Ⓐ Your room is a pig pen. How do you even find your bed?
Ⓑ It has rained cats and dogs all day long. I wish the rain would stop.
Ⓒ Our math home work was a breeze.
Ⓓ I could not eat Susan's biscuits because they were as hard as a rock.

Question Number: 28   RL.4.4

Janice is such an angel means that Janice:

Ⓐ is mean
Ⓑ is annoying
Ⓒ is kind
Ⓓ has wings

NOTES

Question Number: 29   RL.4.4

Jimmy is an ox.
The metaphor 'is an ox' means what?

Ⓐ   He is weak.
Ⓑ   He is blind.
Ⓒ   He is strong.
Ⓓ   He is deaf.

Question Number: 30   RL.4.4

Linda is a road hog. She drives too fast.
What is the metaphor in the sentence above?

Ⓐ   She drives too fast.
Ⓑ   She is a road hog.
Ⓒ   Linda is.
Ⓓ   She drives.

Question Number: 31   RL.4.5

Which text structure is used in the classic story "The Three Little Pigs?"

Ⓐ   Cause and effect
Ⓑ   Compare and contrast
Ⓒ   Problem and solution
Ⓓ   Sequence or chronological

I saw the most unusual chair in a furniture store today while walking around the mall. The chair was shaped like a high-heel shoe. The seat was created from the toe of the shoe, and the high heel and back of the shoe created the chair's back. Hot pink velvet covered the top portion of the shoe chair. Black velvet covered the bottom and heel of the shoe chair. Along the sides of the toes and heel, huge rhinestones were glued onto the velvet. I wonder who would want a chair like that.

Question Number: 32   RL.4.5

What is the structure of the above text?

Ⓐ   Cause and effect
Ⓑ   Compare and contrast
Ⓒ   Problem and solution
Ⓓ   Description

Beau was a nine-year-old boy who wanted a pet dog very badly. Every day, he asked his parents for a dog. They always told him no, because they didn't think he was responsible enough to take care of a dog. One day, Beau made a deal with his parents. He told them that he would keep his room clean and do other household chores for an entire month to prove he was responsible enough to have a pet. That is exactly what he did, and his parents got him a fluffy, white puppy he named Snow White.

Question Number: 33   **RL.4.5**

What is the text structure of this passage?

Ⓐ Description
Ⓑ Cause and Effect
Ⓒ Compare/Contrast
Ⓓ Problem/Solution

Read the two passages and answer the questions that follow.

Passage 1

"The Elephant Who Saw the World," Mary started speaking. It was Friday, and the students had to share their creative writing stories of the week.

Mary loved writing, and this part of the week, when they were able to make up stories for creative writing, was her favorite part. She enjoyed it so much she became really good at it. When she was home on the weekends and she didn't have much homework, she would sit in her room for hours and create stories to share with her friends and family. Her parents always supported her and were her biggest fans.

However, there was one part about every Friday at school that Mary did not enjoy, and that was when she had to share her story in front of the class. The teacher made all of the children share on Friday afternoons, and this made Mary very nervous. She was shy, and although she knew her teacher was right, she didn't like it.

After sitting and listening to the other children share, Mary finally heard her name called. She knew it was her turn to share. She got out of her seat slowly, walked to the front of the room and began.

Passage 2

Timmy grabbed his paper and ran to the front of the classroom. Today was the day! He was so excited to finally have a chance to tell his story. He loved writing and his mind swam with ideas but he couldn't seem to get them all out. For weeks, he had worked and worked so hard to get the right words down on the page.

Finally, during writing time this week, his ideas gelled and the words flowed, creating the most exciting piece of work possible. His story was sure to capture the minds of his classmates and they would want him to tell stories again and again. He was even ready to read the story aloud, having practiced different voices for the different characters and parts of the story.

As he sat and listened to the other children, he bubbled over with excitement and anticipation. Hearing his name, he jumped up and ran to the front of the classroom. "Long ago," Timmy began, "a spaceship came and landed on my grandfather's barn…"

Question Number: 34   **RL.4.5**

How does the description of Mary and Timmy's emotions add to the story?

Ⓐ Describing their emotions and feelings allows the reader to connect with both characters.
Ⓑ Describing their thoughts needs more dialogue.
Ⓒ The words and phrases the author uses deepens the description of the classroom.
Ⓓ The descriptions allow the reader to see that Timmy is too shy to read his story but does it anyway.

When I was little my mom gave me a diary. She told me that it was something really personal and special and I could use it to write down all my thoughts and ideas. She said some famous people kept diaries and when they died, their diary was published into a book. Anne Frank is someone who did this. She lived in the Netherlands but was originally from Germany. During the time of World War II, a group called the Nazis were in power in Germany; they did not like Jews. Anne and her family were Jewish so they had to hide. Her diary tells the story of their time when they lived in hiding.

Question Number: 35   **RL.4.5**

What is the structure of this text?

Ⓐ Chronological
Ⓑ Cause and Effect
Ⓒ Descriptive
Ⓓ Problem and Solution

You are not the kind of guy who would be at a place like this at this time of the morning. But here you are, and you cannot say that the terrain is entirely unfamiliar, although the details are fuzzy. —Opening lines of Jay McInerney's Bright Lights, Big City (1984)

Question Number: 36   RL.4.6

The above passage uses which style of narration?

Ⓐ First person
Ⓑ Second person
Ⓒ Third person
Ⓓ Fourth person

You didn't want to ask for a loan, but you had no choice. You spent all of your allowance at the ball-game, and now you don't have the money to buy your mom a birthday present.

Question Number: 37   RL.4.6

The above passage uses which style of narration?

Ⓐ First person
Ⓑ Second person
Ⓒ Third person
Ⓓ Fourth person

Max went for a ride in the park. While on his ride, he saw his best friend. They decided to go to the movies instead of riding in the park. Max called his mom and asked if it would be alright to go to the movie with his friend. She said yes, so Max and Sammy jumped on their bikes and went to see *Superman*.

Question Number: 38   RL.4.6

The above passage uses which style of narration?

Ⓐ First person
Ⓑ Second person
Ⓒ Third person
Ⓓ Fourth person

I wanted to learn how to knit, so I asked my grandmother to teach me. She agreed, so I went to the store and bought yarn and knitting needles. I had my first lesson last week. I quickly learned that knitting is much harder than I thought it would be. I don't think I want to learn to knit anymore.

Question Number: 39   RL.4.6

The above passage uses which style of narration?

Ⓐ First person
Ⓑ Second person
Ⓒ Third person
Ⓓ Fourth person

I wonder why Mindy didn't come to the meeting. Did I forget to tell her about? Did she forget about it? I think I will call her and see why she isn't here.

Question Number: 40   RL.4.6

The above passage uses which style of narration?

Ⓐ First person
Ⓑ Second person
Ⓒ Third person
Ⓓ Fourth person

Question Number: 41   **RL.4.7**

Which text below best represents what is happening in the picture?

Ⓐ Thelma watched her two baby lions, Louis and Lisa as they played. They were playing well until they started fighting over something the zoo keeper had thrown into the enclosure.

Ⓑ Thelma watched her two baby meerkats, Louis and Lisa, as they played. They were playing well until they started fighting over something the zoo keeper had thrown into the enclosure.

Ⓒ Thelma watched her two baby monkeys, Louis and Lisa, as they played. They were playing well until they started fighting over something the zoo keeper had thrown into the enclosure.

Ⓓ Thelma watched her two baby koala bears, Louis and Lisa, as they played. They were playing well until they started fighting over something the zoo keeper had thrown into the enclosure.

Question Number: 42   **RL.4.7**

Which paragraph would be an appropriate description for the picture above?

Ⓐ One day last spring I was out walking as it was a beautiful spring day. I came across an empty forest and heard a noise. It sounded like a baby but it couldn't have been a baby since there was no one else there. I walked over to where I thought the noise was coming from and stopped in front of a large hollow tree. It looked as if it had been there for a very long time. I stopped and listened. I heard the noise again and it was definitely coming from inside the tree. I looked inside and I saw a little kitten.

Ⓑ One day last spring I was out walking as it was a beautiful spring day. I came across an empty parking lot and heard a noise. It sounded like a baby but it couldn't have been a baby since there was no one else there. I walked over to where I thought the noise was coming from and stopped in front of a large box. It looked like some thing someone may have used for moving. I stopped and listened. I heard the noise again and it was definitely coming from inside the box. I looked inside and I saw a little kitten.

Ⓒ One day last spring I was out walking as it was a beautiful spring day. I came across a construction site and heard a noise. It sounded like a baby but it couldn't have been a baby since there was no one else there. I walked over to where I thought the noise was coming from and stopped in front of a large cement pipe. It looked like some thing they might use to transport water underground. I stopped and listened. I heard the noise again and it was definitely coming from inside the pipe. I looked inside and I saw a little kitten.

Ⓓ At first the kitten was scared but eventually, with lots of coaxing, came to one of the open ends of the tree. I was able to see that it was a little black and white kitten who was probably very hungry and scared. I took the kitten home and it became my companion from that day on.

Question Number: 43   **RL.4.7**

Which of the statements below most accurately reflects the picture?

Ⓐ   Many people like to act, even if they don't act very well. Acting helps them express how they are feeling. Sometimes acting makes them feel happy. Not everyone wants to be a professional, though. Professional actors like to entertain other people. Their skill is usually a combination of talent and training.

Ⓑ   Many people like to dance, even if they don't dance very well. Dancing helps them express how they are feeling. Sometimes dancing makes them feel happy. Not every one wants to be a professional, though. Professional dancers like to entertain other people. Their skill is usually a combination of talent and training.

Ⓒ   Many people like to sing, even if they don't sing very well. Singing helps them express how they are feeling. Sometimes singing makes them feel happy. Not everyone wants to be a professional, though. Professional singers use their voices to entertain other people. Their skill is usually a combination of talent and training.

Ⓓ   Their skill is usually a combination of talent and training. Most professional dancers work with a coach. They usually start training at a young age. Many of them get their first experience by being in school musicals. Talent and training are not enough to make a successful career, though. Young people who want to be dancers should also have poise, good stage presence, creativity, and the ability to deal with change. They must be healthy and strong, too.

Question Number: 44   **RL.4.7**

Which paragraph would be an appropriate description for the picture above?

Ⓐ Summer is probably my favorite season. One of my most favorite things to do is to
     go watch a sandcastle building contest they have every year in San Diego, California.
     We can see amazing sandcastles that people spend hours and days building. This
     year one of the winners of the contest made this really large superhero to honor their
     love of comic books.

Ⓑ Summer is probably my favorite season. One of my most favorite things to do is to go
     watch a sandcastle building contest they have every year in San Diego, California.
     We can see amazing sandcastles that people spend hours and days building. This
     year one of the winners of the contest made this really long snake to honor their
     Mexican heritage.

Ⓒ Summer is probably my favorite season. One of my most favorite things to do is to
     go watch a sandcastle building contest they have every year in San Diego, California.
     We can see amazing sandcastles that people spend hours and days building. This
     year one of the winners of the contest made this really big pyramid to honor their
     Egyptian heritage.

Ⓓ Summer is probably my favorite season. One of my most favorite things to do is to
     go watch a sandcastle building contest they have every year in San Diego, California.
     We can see amazing sandcastles that people spend hours and days building. This
     year one of the winners of the contest made this really long dragon to honor their
     Chinese heritage.

100

"Good morning boys and girls," said Mrs. Miller. "We are going to try something new today. It is called Echo Reading. This is a new reading strategy for our class. During reading time, I will read aloud two or three sentences while you follow along silently. Then, you will read aloud the same sentences I just read."

Question Number: 45   RL.4.7

What would be an important picture or illustration to use with this paragraph?

Ⓐ a book
Ⓑ a teacher and student looking at the same book
Ⓒ a classroom full of students
Ⓓ a pencil and paper

The Man, the Hawk, and the Dove

LONG AGO IN NIGERIA, there was a man who had been blind and lame all his life. One evening, as he was sitting in front of his house, he couldn't help but feel sorry for himself. After all, he couldn't walk or see.

All of a sudden, a dove flew into his robe.

"Save me," the dove whispered urgently.

Then a hawk whished up and stopped in front of the man. "This dove is mine," squawked the hawk.

The man gripped the robe tightly.

"I beg you, you don't know how terribly hungry I am," said the hawk. "If I don't have that dove, I will die. I am a hawk and you know that we must eat what we can." Then he straightened up and said, "Hawks see for miles around. If you release the dove to me, I'll share the secret of how your eyesight can be restored."

The man hesitated. After all, wasn't it true that the basic nature of all things is that one beast hunts another?

"You mustn't listen to that hawk!" chirped the dove frantically. "If you save me from certain death, I'll tell you how your legs can be healed so you can walk."

What was he to do? Fortunately, the footsteps of his best friend were approaching.

"Should I gain my sight, or my legs?" he asked his friend.

The friend was silent. "Well," he said at last, "you have to paddle your own canoe. I can't help you decide this one."

"The next time you ask, I'll be sure to give you good advice, too!" the man called out as his friend walked quickly away.

Question Number: 46   **RL.4.7**

What image would help the reader understand the moral of the fable?

Ⓐ   The dove flying into the man's coat
Ⓑ   The hawk talking to the man
Ⓒ   The man talking to his friend
Ⓓ   The friend walking away from the man

Question Number: 47   **RL.4.7**

What caption would best help the readers understand the image above from Treasure Island?

Ⓐ   "Livesey," returned the squire, "you are always in the right of it. I'll be as silent as the grave."
Ⓑ   The doctor opened the seals with great care, and there fell out the map of an island
Ⓒ   I said good-bye to Mother and the cove, and the dear old Admiral Benbow
Ⓓ   On our little walk along the quays, he made himself the most interesting companion

102

Read the two passages and answer the questions that follow.

Passage 1

"The Elephant Who Saw the World," Mary started speaking. It was Friday, and the students had to share their creative writing stories of the week.

Mary loved writing, and this part of the week, when they were able to make up stories for creative writing, was her favorite part. She enjoyed it so much she became really good at it. When she was home on the weekends and she didn't have much homework, she would sit in her room for hours and create stories to share with her friends and family. Her parents always supported her and were her biggest fans.

However, there was one part about every Friday at school that Mary did not enjoy, and that was when she had to share her story in front of the class. The teacher made all of the children share on Friday afternoons, and this made Mary very nervous. She was shy, and although she knew her teacher was right, she didn't like it.

After sitting and listening to the other children share, Mary finally heard her name called. She knew it was her turn to share. She got out of her seat slowly, walked to the front of the room and began.

Passage 2

Timmy grabbed his paper and ran to the front of the classroom. Today was the day! He was so excited to finally have a chance to tell his story. He loved writing and his mind swam with ideas but he couldn't seem to get them all out. For weeks, he had worked and worked so hard to get the right words down on the page.

Finally, during writing time this week, his ideas gelled and the words flowed, creating the most exciting piece of work possible. His story was sure to capture the minds of his classmates and they would want him to tell stories again and again. He was even ready to read the story aloud, having practiced different voices for the different characters and parts of the story.

As he sat and listened to the other children, he bubbled over with excitement and anticipation. Hearing his name, he jumped up and ran to the front of the classroom. "Long ago," Timmy began, "a spaceship came and landed on my grandfather's barn…"

Question Number: 48   **RL.4.7**

If you were to create a Venn Diagram of Mary's and Timmy's experiences with their writing assignment, what would go in the intersecting circle?

Ⓐ Loved writing
Ⓑ Did not want to share with class
Ⓒ Could not wait to share with class
Ⓓ Wrote a fiction story

Timmy grabbed his paper and ran to the front of the classroom. Today was the day! He was so excited to finally have a chance to tell his story. He loved writing and his mind swam with ideas but he couldn't seem to get them all out. For weeks, he had worked and worked so hard to get the right words down on the page.

Finally, during writing time this week, his ideas gelled and the words flowed, creating the most exciting piece of work possible. His story was sure to capture the minds of his classmates and they would want him to tell stories again and again. He was even ready to read the story aloud, having practiced different voices for the different characters and parts of the story.

As he sat and listened to the other children, he bubbled over with excitement and anticipation. Hearing his name, he jumped up and ran to the front of the classroom. "Long ago," Timmy began, "a spaceship came and landed on my grandfather's barn..."

Question Number: 49   **RL.4.7**

What image could Timmy include to add depth to his story?

Ⓐ

Ⓒ

Ⓑ

Ⓓ

Read all three passages and answer the questions that follow

Passage 1:

Timothy

Timothy got a job walking dogs each morning. When school started this year, everyone encouraged him to quit his job, but he decided to keep it. He knew it would be hard to get up every morning at 5 a.m. in order to get all of the dogs walked and then go to school all day. In addition, he plans to sing in the chorus, play basketball, and be a mentor in the tutoring program this year. He knows it will not be easy, but he thinks his hard work will be worth it. He is trying to save enough money to go to a youth camp next summer.

Passage 2:

Adam likes to spend time with his friends. If he is not with them, he is texting them or playing games with them online. Adam is always busy. He cannot stand to sit around and do nothing. In fact, the only time he is still is when he is sleeping. Adam plays football, basketball, soccer, and baseball. He loves to be involved in whatever is going on at school or at the town's youth center. He spends a lot of his time encouraging people to recycle and even volunteers at the youth center. Although he loves spending time with his friends, he is willing to give up time with them to help others.

Passage 3

Stanley loves to stay at home. He enjoys activities that can be done alone such as reading, drawing, and spending time with his dogs. Most days after school you can find him at home enjoying one of his favorite activities. He also thinks recycling is important and makes sure his family does it. Although he likes being alone, he enjoys volunteering at the youth center with his brother. He thinks it is important to make a difference in the lives others, which is why he thinks he would like to be a doctor. Adam and Stanley may be different in many ways, but they join together and make a difference in their community.

Question Number: 50   **RL.4.9**

If you compare Timothy and Adam, which statement is correct?

Ⓐ Timothy participates in extracurricular activities, but Adam does not.
Ⓑ Timothy does not participate in extracurricular activities, but Adam does.
Ⓒ Timothy and Adam both participate in extracurricular activities.
Ⓓ Neither Timothy nor Adam participates in extracurricular activities.

NOTES

Question Number: 51   RL.4.9

If you contrast Timothy and Stanley, which statement is correct?

Ⓐ Stanley participates in many extracurricular activities such as sports and chorus, but Timothy does not.
Ⓑ Stanley and Timothy both participate in extracurricular activities such as sports and chorus.
Ⓒ Neither Stanley nor Timothy participates in extracurricular activities.
Ⓓ Stanley enjoys solitary activities such as drawing, but Timothy enjoys group activities such as chorus and sports.

Question Number: 52   RL.4.9

Compare and contrast Adam and his brother Stanley. Which statement is true?

Ⓐ Both Adam and Stanley believe in recycling.
Ⓑ Neither Adam nor Stanley believes in recycling.
Ⓒ Adam believes in recycling, but Stanley does not.
Ⓓ Adam does not believe in recycling, but Stanley does.

Lindsay, Scarlet, and Austin loved their aunts and were really excited. They ran upstairs and started getting their things together to take with them. They put everything in one bag that they would have to take to school with them. They were going to stay with Aunt Margaret for two nights and the last night with their Auntie Josephine.

At the end of the school day, the children came running out of classroom doors from all different directions. Aunt Margaret was waiting for her nieces and nephew at the entrance to the school. She was wearing a bright red suit with a sparkly cat pin on it. She also had on a proper wool hat to match. She noticed a scuff on her shoes when her nieces and nephew ran up to her.

She cried, "Oh, my goodness! I am so happy you are here. The children at your school are just a bunch of hooligans. I was nearly trampled while I was standing here! Let's go get in the car." Aunt Margaret pointed to a large, green four-door station wagon parked in the lot.

The next day, a funny-sounding honk came from the front of the house. The children ran outside and saw Auntie Jo sitting in her convertible. She was wearing a big cowboy hat. She wore a pair of polka dot shorts with a too large shirt.

Question Number: 53   RL.4.9

Compare and contrast the way the two different aunts dressed.

Ⓐ Auntie Jo and Aunt Margaret dressed the same.
Ⓑ Auntie Jo dressed very casually while Aunt Margaret dressed very properly.
Ⓒ Auntie Jo was wearing a skirt and Aunt Margaret was wearing a dress.
Ⓓ None of the above

Question Number: 54   RL.4.9

Compare and contrast the cars that the aunts drove.

Ⓐ Auntie Jo had a convertible, and Aunt Margaret had a station wagon.
Ⓑ The two aunts had the same car.
Ⓒ Auntie Jo had a sedan, and Aunt Margaret had a convertible.
Ⓓ Neither Aunt liked to wear skirts or dresses.

The red tail hawks noticed something was happening to all the other animals living in Running Brook during the spring. The birds seemed to be losing their feathers. The bears were losing their fur. Mountain goats were complaining that their feet hurt. The beavers had cavities, and the deer all seemed to be catching colds. The red squirrels had gotten so fat they almost could not make it across the road.

Hawk made an observation. He was pretty sure that everything started happening when the town's first fast food restaurant opened. Forest Fawn thought he brought a great idea to the town and that he could make some extra money by opening a place to eat something quickly. Forest Fawn knew how difficult it was to find food during winter months. He thought he was doing his friends a favor.

The restaurant sold birdseed in five different flavors. For the bears, Forest Fawn sold artificially flavored honey and salmon cakes and deep-fried berries. Salted tree moss with lichen-flavored chips was on the shelf for the mountain goats and deer.

Question Number: 55   RL.4.9

What was Hawk's theory of what was causing the animals' compaints?

Ⓐ Birds were losing their feathers, and bears were losing patches of fur.
Ⓑ Beavers got cavities, and deer had colds.
Ⓒ Bad things were happening to the animals because of the food they were eating.
Ⓓ The squirrels were getting fat and the mountain goats complained about their feet.

Question Number: 56   RL.4.9

Compare what happened to the beavers and the birds.

Ⓐ The birds lost their feathers, and the beavers had cavities.
Ⓑ Tthe birds had colds, and the beavers lost their fur.
Ⓒ The birds liked the candy, and the beavers liked the syrup
Ⓓ The birds had sore feet and the beavers gained weight.

If you join our music club, you will receive 4 free CDs. These CDs are yours to keep even if you decide to cancel your membership. If you choose to stay a member and buy just 2 CDs at regular price, you will get to choose 3 more CDs to keep for free. After your first purchase you will receive 10 points for every CD you buy after that. When you collect 30 points, you get to choose another free CD! If you want to earn even more free CDs, then have your friends join, too. When a friend joins and gives your name, you will get 3 more free CDs. The best part is that you get 3 free CDs each time you have another friend join our club, so join today and start collecting your favorite CDs.

Question Number: 57   RI.4.1

What detail from the text encourages music club members to get their friends to join the club?

Ⓐ "If you join our music club, you will receive 4 free CDs."
Ⓑ "After your first purchase you will receive 10 points for every
     CD you buy after that."
Ⓒ "If you want to earn even more free CDs, then have your friends join, too."
Ⓓ "The best part is that you get 3 free CDs each time you have another
     friend join our club, so join today and start collecting your favorite CDs."

Do you like frogs? Do you know what a spring peeper is?

Spring peepers are tiny little tree frogs that live in wooded areas near ponds. Although these little frogs are tiny, only about an inch big, they make a very loud sound. They are found mostly in the central and eastern parts of the United States. So, when the weather begins to get warmer after winter, these little frogs start to sing. Their "peep," which is why they are called spring peepers, can be heard for miles around. They live near ponds so they can lay their eggs in the water.

When the weather starts getting colder again, the spring peepers start to go into hiding. They hibernate under logs or any other place they can find in the forest to protect them from the cold. For example, sometimes they hide under fallen leaves or even in a small hole in the ground.

109

Question Number: 58   **RI.4.1**

Which paragraph contains details that support Monique's idea that people are most likely to see spring peepers during warm weather months?

Ⓐ Paragraphs 1 and 2
Ⓑ Paragraphs 1 and 3
Ⓒ Paragraph 3
Ⓓ Paragraphs 2 and 3

Did you know that the coconut tree is very useful to people? Each and every part of the tree can be used for a many different things. For example, the coconut fruit, which we get from the tree, is very nutritious and is used in cooking many different kinds of food. Coconut milk, which is taken from the coconut, tastes very delicious. It is used to prepare a variety of sweet dishes.

Oil can be extracted from a dried coconut. Coconut oil is a very good moisturizer. It is used in many beauty products like body wash, face wash, shampoos and conditioners. The oil is also used for cooking some of the tropical foods. Some coconut trees grow straight and tall, and some trees are very short. Coconut trees do not have branches. They have long leaves which grow right at the top of the tree. The leaves are used for many different things. Leaf ribs are made into brooms, and fiber is obtained from the outer cover of the nut and used for mattresses, rugs, etc. The trunk is used to make logs for small boats. It is also used for firewood. The sweet water of the tender coconut quenches the thirst during the hot summer months and is also very healthy.

Question Number: 59   RI.4.2

What is the most appropriate title for this passage?

Ⓐ   The Coconut Tree and Its Uses
Ⓑ   The Coconut Tree
Ⓒ   Things We Get from the Coconut
Ⓓ   Tall Coconut Trees

Pollution hurts the world around us. It upsets the balance of nature, which is very important for our survival. The problems in the environment come in four ways. These affect the soil, water, air and sound around us. Large amounts of trash from factories and houses can cause land pollution. Chemicals used in farming also pollute the soil. Plastics are also major waste products. Too many animals needing to eat and the cutting down of trees creates deserts and wastelands. Deserts already cover 40 percent of the Earth's surface. Harmful waste in water makes it unhealthy for humans and animals. Plants and animals in the water are often harmed because of the thousands of tons of oil that get spilled into the seas and oceans. The air that we breathe is dirtied by smoke and dust in the atmosphere. Lung illnesses are common when the air is polluted. Noise pollution in cities has grown beyond what many people can stand. Pollution is becoming a serious problem for the whole world.

Question Number: 60   RI.4.2

Which detail in the above passage tells us that the soil is being polluted?

Ⓐ   the oil spills in the seas and oceans.
Ⓑ   smoke and dust in the air
Ⓒ   large amounts of trash from factories and houses
Ⓓ   global warming

People who travel on business are usually reimbursed for their travel expenses; that is, they are repaid for money they have spent for the company.

Question Number: 61   RI.4.4

What word in the sentence above helps you understand what reimburse means?

Ⓐ   expenses
Ⓑ   representatives
Ⓒ   repaid
Ⓓ   business

Many years ago there were no self-serve grocery stores unlike today. Shoppers were served by clerks who chose everything for them. When the first self-serve market was opened, no one thought that it would be successful. Owners of the full-service grocery stores laughed at the idea and said the public would probably <u>boycott</u> the stores.

But Clarence Saunders, the man who came up with this new idea, thought he could save some money by having shoppers help themselves from the open shelves. He was warned by many of his competitors that customers would <u>boycott</u> his new type of grocery store and put him out of business.

Question Number: 62   **RI.4.4**

What is the meaning of the word boycott in the above text?

Ⓐ to only go to this store and shop there
Ⓑ to get a lot of money
Ⓒ to lose a lot of money
Ⓓ to refuse to buy something

We get a lot of copra from the Malay Peninsula. Copra is dried coconut meat which is used for making coconut oil. We use coconut oil for cooking and as an ingredient many beauty products.

Question Number: 63   **RI.4.4**

Which words in the above text help to understand the meaning of copra?

Ⓐ coconut oil
Ⓑ coconut meat
Ⓒ Malay Peninsula
Ⓓ beauty products

The first review of *Despicable Me* was <u>favorable</u>. Many people attended and enjoyed the movie.

Question Number: 64   **RI.4.4**

What is the meaning of the underlined word?

Ⓐ clear
Ⓑ negative
Ⓒ positive
Ⓓ unsure

Grandma's Chocolate Cake
1 ¾ cups all-purpose flour
2 cups white sugar
2 sticks of room temperature butter
2 eggs
¾ cup cocoa powder
1 cup milk
1 tsp. vanilla extract
1 tsp. salt

Preheat oven to 350 degrees F.
Butter and flour two 8-inch cake pans.
Combine eggs, sugar, milk, vanilla extract, and butter. Beat until smooth.
Sift together the flour, salt, and cocoa powder.
Slowly add the sifted dry ingredients to the wet ingredients.
Mix until batter is smooth.
Pour the batter into the floured and greased cake pans.
Bake for 35 to 40 minutes.
Cool in pans on cooling rack for 30 minutes.
Ice cake with your favorite frosting.

Question Number: 65   RI.4.5

Which text structure is used in the second half of the above recipe?

Ⓐ Cause and effect
Ⓑ Compare and contrast
Ⓒ Problem and solution
Ⓓ Sequence

Question Number: 66   RI.4.5

If the title of an essay was, "Should Students be Allowed to Have Cell Phones in Elementary School?" what type of writing would it be?

Ⓐ Comparative
Ⓑ Informative
Ⓒ Narrative
Ⓓ Persuasive

Question Number: 67   **RI.4.5**

If the title of an essay is, "Allowing Students to have Cell Phones in Elementary Versus Middle Schools" what type of writing will it be?

Ⓐ Comparative
Ⓑ Informative
Ⓒ Narrative
Ⓓ Persuasive

Question Number: 68   **RI.4.5**

If the title of an essay is, "The Pros and Cons of Wearing School Uniforms," what type of writing will it be?

Ⓐ Comparative
Ⓑ Informative
Ⓒ Narrative
Ⓓ Persuasive

The Parade: A Firsthand Account

When I got there I was dressed from head to toe in sparkly sequins and itchy tights, and I held my baton like a pro. I lined up with others in my squad and we began marching through the streets while the marching band played in front of us. I saw the crowds of people waving and smiling as we passed. Their happy faces made me feel somehow less cold, but by the second mile those happy faces could not soothe the blisters on my feet. I threw my twirling baton into the air, and this time I did not catch it. In fact, when I turned to retrieve it, I tripped the girl behind me and caused quite a situation. I was so embarrassed that I contemplated never showing my face again.

The Parade: A Secondhand Account

I read about the Thanksgiving parade in our school newspaper today. It was held downtown last Saturday morning to honor the American holiday that occurs every year on the third Thursday in November. There was a marching band, floats from all the local businesses, a step team, a ballet studio, and baton twirlers. The temperature outside was forty five degrees, but the sun was shining brightly to help warm over 600 people who came out to see the parade. All in all, the parade was a huge success, and the city plans to hold it again next year.

Question Number: 69   RI.4.6

How is the focus of the firsthand account different from the secondhand account?

Ⓐ The firsthand account focuses on the parade itself, while the secondhand account focuses on the weather on the day of the parade.
Ⓑ The firsthand account has a wide focus that represents the parade as a whole, while the secondhand account is narrow and only talks about the crowd who attended the parade.
Ⓒ The firsthand account is more accurate, while the secondhand account is based on rumor.
Ⓓ The firsthand account focuses only on the personal experience of the speaker, while the secondhand account gives general information from the newspaper report about the parade.

Question Number: 70   RI.4.6

How are the firsthand account and the secondhand account the same?

Ⓐ They both consider the parade a huge success.
Ⓑ They both give specific information about the number of people in attendance.
Ⓒ They both discuss the baton twirlers' sequin costumes.
Ⓓ They both discuss the weather, the marching band, the baton twirlers, and the crowd.

Question Number: 71   RI.4.6

How are the firsthand account and the secondhand account different?

Ⓐ The firsthand account is more personal and includes the speaker's feelings about the parade, while the secondhand account is more objective and includes mostly facts about the parade.
Ⓑ The firsthand account includes more details about the parade, while the secondhand account is more of a broad summary.
Ⓒ The firsthand account is true, while the secondhand account gives false information.
Ⓓ The firsthand account discusses the origins of the parade, while the secondhand account is from a newspaper.

The Inauguration of Barack Obama: A Firsthand Account

When Barack Obama was inaugurated as America's first African-American president, I was watching from my TV only a couple of miles away. It was a cold, cold, cloudy day, but thousands and thousands of people climbed on jam-packed metro train cars, and busses. Some even walked across the Key Bridge from Arlington Virginia to get into Washington, D.C. I saw groups of people moving down the street outside my apartment in their puffy jackets. They had homemade signs and happy faces. I wondered what they would all eat. I also wondered where they would use the bathroom and spend the night. I watched from the warmth of my living room with what I imagined was a much better view of our new President taking the oath of office.

The Inauguration of Barak Obama: A Secondhand Account

Barak Obama was inaugurated as our nation's 44th president on Tuesday, January 20, 2009. It was the most attended event in Washington, D.C.'s history. They inauguration was held during the celebration of the 200th year of Abraham Lincoln's birthday. So, there were many mentions of Lincoln throughout the event. Obama was even sworn into office using the same Bible Lincoln used when he became President.

In addition to welcoming remarks, the oath of office, and an inaugural address, there was also music by Aretha Franklin and Yo Yo Ma among others. The night was celebrated with a series of inaugural balls, which the new First Family attended.

Question Number: 72   **RI.4.6**

How are the two accounts similar?

Ⓐ They both detail the events of election night.
Ⓑ They both give important details about the inauguration itself.
Ⓒ They both tell true events on the day of Barack Obama's first inauguration.
Ⓓ They both talk about the importance of Abraham Lincoln.

Question Number: 73   **RI.4.6**

How are the two accounts different?

Ⓐ The details in the secondhand account may not be accurate, while the details in the firsthand account have been verified to be true.
Ⓑ The secondhand account is more personal than the firsthand account.
Ⓒ The firsthand account is longer than the secondhand account.
Ⓓ The details in the first account are limited only to what the speaker witnessed, while the secondhand account gives more specific details concerning the inauguration.

Question Number: 74   **RI.4.6**

What is the difference in focus between the two accounts?

Ⓐ The first account focuses on the practical details concerning the people in attendance, while the secondhand account focuses on the details of the inauguration event.

Ⓑ The firsthand account focuses on the important details, while the secondhand account is more focused on unimportant details.

Ⓒ The secondhand account focuses on biographical details about Obama's life, while the firsthand account focuses on details like the music that played at the inauguraion.

Ⓓ Both accounts have the same focus.

John Glenn's Return to Space: a Firsthand Account

President Bill Clinton, The White House, Washington, D. C.

Dear Mr. President,
        This is certainly a first for me, writing to a President from space, and it may be a first for you in receiving an E mail direct from an orbiting spacecraft.

        In any event, I want to personally thank you and Mrs. Clinton for coming to the Cape to see the launch. I hope you enjoyed it just half as much as we did on board.. It is truly an awesome experience from a personal standpoint, and of even greater importance for all of the great research projects we have on Discovery. The whole crew was impressed that you would be the first President to personally see a shuttle launch and asked me to include their best regards to you and Hillary.   She has discussed her interest in the space program with Annie on several occasions, and I know she would like to be on a flight just like this.

        We have gone almost a third of the way around the world in the time it has taken me to write this letter, and the rest of the crew is waiting. Again, our thanks and best regards. Will try to give you a personal briefing after we return next Saturday.

    Sincerely,

                    John Glenn

Margie S. Keller
Admin Officer
Astronaut Office
281-244-8991

John Glenn's Return to Space: a Secondhand Account

In October of 1998, John Glenn returned to space aboard the space shuttle Discovery. It was on that mission that the first American to orbit the Earth made history again by becoming the oldest man to fly in space. He was a sitting U.S. Senator from Ohio at the time. President Bill Clinton attended the launch as the first U.S. President to do so.

Question Number: 75   RI.4.6

What is the difference in focus between the firsthand and secondhand account above?

Ⓐ The firsthand account and the secondhand account have the same focus.
Ⓑ The firsthand account is more accurate than the secondhand account.
Ⓒ The firsthand account focuses on providing information to President Bill Clinton, while
     the secondhand account focuses on details about John Glenn.
Ⓓ The firsthand account is an actual letter and the second is as well.

Question Number: 76   RI.4.6

How are the two accounts similar?

Ⓐ They both give information about President Clinton being the first U.S. President to personally
     see a launch.
Ⓑ They both include information about the date of the historic mission.
Ⓒ They both detail the important research being conducted on the mission.
Ⓓ The firsthand account is an article and the second is an actual letter.

Question Number: 77   RI.4.6

How are the two accounts different?

Ⓐ The firsthand account is a letter and tells a little bit about Glenn's personal
     experience, while the secondhand account is an informational paragraph and was
     most likely written by someone who did not even know Glenn.
Ⓑ The firsthand account discusses John Glenn's return to space in 1998, while the
     secondhand account discusses Glenn's first orbit around Earth in 1962.
Ⓒ The firsthand account is written in complete sentences, while the secondhand account
     is written in short, note-like form.
Ⓓ The firsthand account is an article and the second is an actual letter.

NOTES

Question Number: 78   **RI.4.6**

What is the difference between a firsthand account and secondhand account of an event or occurance?

Ⓐ Firsthand accounts are written by people who witness an event first, while second hand accounts are written by people who witness the event second.

Ⓑ Firsthand accounts are written by people who witnessed the event, while secondhand accounts are written by people who learned details of the event from other sources.

Ⓒ Firsthand accounts are true, while secondhand accounts are usually made up.

Ⓓ Firsthand accounts are primary documents and secondhand accounts are not.

The following excerpt is from the November 12, 1892 edition of "Golden Days" magazine. It explains how condensed milk was made:

The processes employed are very simple, the fresh milk being put into a great copper tank with a steam jacket. While it is being heated sugar is added, and the mixture is then drawn off into a vacuum tank, where evaporation is produced by heat.

The vacuum tank will hold, perhaps, nine thousand quarts. It has a glass window at the top, through which the operator in charge looks from time to time. He can tell by the appearance of the milk when the time has arrived to shut off the steam, and this must be done at just the right moment, else the batch will be spoiled.

Next the condensed milk is drawn into forty-quart cans, which are set in very cold spring water, where they are made to revolve rapidly by a mechanical contrivance in order that their contents may cool evenly.

When the water does not happen to be cold enough, ice is put in to bring it down to the proper temperature. Finally the tin cans of market size are filled with the milk by a machine, which pours into each one exactly sixteen ounces automatically, one girl shoving the cans beneath the spout, while another removes them as fast as they are filled.

Question Number: 79   **RI.4.7**

Which text feature would be most helpful for the reader to understand the process of making condensed milk?

Ⓐ a numbered list of steps with illustrations for each step

Ⓑ a timeline of the events in the process

Ⓒ a map of where evaporated milk was made in 1892

Ⓓ a picture of an evaporated milk can

120

BETWEEN WOOD AND FIELD. Arrangement of wall tents with flys, set up with stakes.

THE TENT "GREEN." Conical wall tents accommodating eight cots. Not easy to put up and give little head room.

Well-built floors keep out ground damp, and make level and steady supports.

Question Number: 80   **RI.4.7**

These photographs and captions are most likely included in which of the following texts?

Ⓐ a recipe book for outdoorsmen
Ⓑ a guide to city life
Ⓒ a guide to Girl Scout camps
Ⓓ a fishing guide

121

Catepillar feeding on a milkweed leaf as it prepares to begin its transition

Catepillar hung up for the change to the chrysalis phase

The transition stage

The chrysalis

Question Number: 81   **RI.4.7**

What would these photographs and captions be most helpful in explaining?

Ⓐ all about plants
Ⓑ a very hungry caterpillar
Ⓒ how a catepillar begins its transformation into a butterfly
Ⓓ how a caterpillar goes to sleep each night

122

Smoking is a nasty habit. It not only damages your health, but it also affects the way you look and even smell. People who smoke have horrible breath that smells like a dirty ashtray, but it is not only their breath that smells bad. Their clothes and hair also smell like smoke, and if this isn't bad enough, smoking causes their teeth to turn yellow.

Question Number: 82   **RI.4.8**

Above is a section from a persuasive essay written to encourage people not to smoke. What evidence does the writer provide that supports the claim that smoking affects the way you look?

Ⓐ   Smoking is a nasty habit.
Ⓑ   People who smoke have horrible breath.
Ⓒ   Their clothes and hair smell like smoke.
Ⓓ   Smoking causes their teeth to turn yellow.

Question Number: 83   **RI.4.8**

Above is a section from a persuasive essay written to encourage people not to smoke. Which statement does NOT provide evidence that supports the claim that smoking causes you smell bad?

Ⓐ   People who smoke have horrible breath that smells like a dirty ashtray.
Ⓑ   Onions also may you cause you to have bad breath.
Ⓒ   but it is not only their breath that smells bad
Ⓓ   Their clothes and hair also smell like smoke.

Drinking alcohol and driving is a dangerous combination. This is because of the way alcohol affects the nervous system. Alcohol can make you act silly and laugh at things that are not funny. Alcohol slows down the brain. This causes the driver to have a slower reaction time and difficulty thinking. It causes them to be unable to make quick, clear decisions about traffic and road conditions. In addition, alcohol's effect on the brain causes a lack of coordination. This can lead a driver to weave on and off the road. It can also cause them to have trouble applying the brakes when needed. Any one of these reactions can easily cause a driver to have an accident that could harm or kill themselves or others.

Question Number: 84   RI.4.8

Above is a section from a persuasive essay written to encourage people not to drink. What statement does NOT provide evidence supporting the writer's claim that drinking alcohol and driving is dangerous?

Ⓐ Alcohol can make you act silly and laugh at things that are not funny.
Ⓑ Alcohol slows down the brain.
Ⓒ Alcohol's effect on the brain causes lack of coordination.
Ⓓ This can lead a driver to weave on and off the road or have trouble applying the brakes when needed.

Dr. Johnson thinks that everyone should take responsiblility for preserving the toad species. By not mowing certain areas of our lawns, special areas of wild grass could be kept for toads. This could possibly help to preserve the species. According to Dr. Johnson, dangerous chemicals found in pesticides and fertilizers are also reasons why the species is starting to disappear. These chemicals have an effect on the food chain and can kill the insects that the toads eat. If we are able to keep a special space in our yards and stop using chemical fertilizers, Dr. Johnson believes that the toads can be saved.

Question Number: 85   RI.4.8

What would be an appropriate title for the above text?

Ⓐ Please Stop Mowing Your Lawn
Ⓑ Don't Let Toads Disappear
Ⓒ Please Stop Using Fertiilizers
Ⓓ Dr. Johnson and the Toad

On the Trail: an Outdoor Book for Girls by Adelia Beard and Lina Beard

For any journey, by rail or by boat, one has a general idea of the direction to be taken, the character of the land or water to be crossed, and of what one will find at the end. So it should be in striking the trail. Learn all you can about the path you are to follow. Whether it is plain or obscure, wet or dry; where it leads; and its length, measured more by time than by actual miles. A smooth, even trail of five miles will not consume the time and strength that must be expended upon a trail of half that length which leads over uneven ground, varied by bogs and obstructed by rocks and fallen trees, or a trail that is all up-hill climbing.

How to Camp Out by John M. Gould

Think over and decide whether you will walk, go horseback, sail, camp out in one place, or what you will do; then learn what you can of the route you propose to go over, or the ground where you intend to camp for the season. If you think of moving through or camping in places unknown to you, it is important to learn whether you can buy provisions and get lodgings along your route. See some one, if you can, who has been where you think of going, [Pg 10]and put down in a note-book all he tells you that is important.

Question Number: 86   **RI.4.9**

Which sentence below integrates information from the above texts?

Ⓐ Hiking over bogs or fallen trees is harder than hiking an even, clear trail.
Ⓑ You should talk to someone who has been where you plan to go so you can get information and tips that will be helpful in planning your camping trip.
Ⓒ Hiking over uneven land will take longer than going the same distance over flat land.
Ⓓ When planning a camping trip, it is important to plan by considering both the type of the trail you will travel and whether you will walk or ride on horseback.

Question Number: 87   **RI.4.9**

Which paragraph below combines information from the above texts?

Ⓐ Camping is terribly difficult, and only true experts should try to camp overnight.
Ⓑ If you plan to camp somewhere you've never been, you should learn everything you can about the trail. Find out what the land is like and where you can buy supplies along the way.
Ⓒ Only boys can go on long camping trips across bogs or uneven land.
Ⓓ You should always take a notebook on your camping trips to write about your trip and draw pictures of plants and animals you see.

Question Number: 88   RI.4.9

Which pair of sentences shows similar information found in both texts?

Ⓐ "Learn all you can about the path you are to follow."
    "Learn what you can of the route you propose to go over."

Ⓑ "So it should be in striking the trail."
    "Think over and decide whether you will walk, go horseback, sail, camp out in one place, or what you will do…"

Ⓒ "A smooth, even trail of five miles will not consume the time and strength that must be expended upon a trail of half that length which leads over uneven ground…"
    "… It is important to learn whether you can buy provisions and get lodgings along your route."

Ⓓ All of the above

The Amazing Peacock

Did you know that the term, "peacock" really only refers to the male of its species? A female peafowl is actually called a "peahen." Peacocks are native to India and other parts of Southeast Asia and are known for their brilliantly colored feathers. Their bodies can be thirty-five to fifty inches, while their beautiful tails can be as long as five feet! People admire peacocks for their beautiful feathers, but they also serve a purpose for the birds. The peacocks' tails help peahens choose their mates!

The Peafowl and It's Magnificent Tail

Peafowl are glorious animals and have long been admired by humans for their beautiful, brightly colored tail feathers. Their tails do not reach their full length until the peacock is four or five years old. When that happens, the peacock will strut day after day in hopes of attracting a mate. Peafowl are actually a kind of pheasant. Some are natives of India, while others come from Sri Lanka, Myanmar (Burma), or Java. Peafowl are some of the largest flying birds around!

Question Number: 89   RI.4.9

Which paragraph below integrates information from both texts above?

Ⓐ The peafowl, more commonly known as the peacock, has beautiful tail feathers. Those feathers can grow to be around five feet long, but their growth usually does not peak until the peacock is four or five years old.
Ⓑ Peacocks are wonderful creatures. They come from India, and their bodies can grow to be thirty-five to fifty inches long.
Ⓒ Peacocks like to strut around all day with their beautiful feathers spread wide for all to see. This is what helps them to find a mate.
Ⓓ None of the above

Question Number: 90   **RI.4.9**

Which sentence below combines information from both texts above?

Ⓐ Peacocks have been admired by humans for over a thousand years because their tail feathers are so beautiful.
Ⓑ "Peafowl" actually refers to both the male and female of its species, while "peacock" is the correct term for the male only.
Ⓒ Peacocks are enormous.
Ⓓ With bodies as big as thirty-five to fifty inches and tails as long as five feet, peacocks are some of the largest flying birds you will ever see.

Sacagawea

Sacagawea is a famous Native American from the Shoshone tribe. She became famous when she helped two men, explorers named Lewis and Clark, find their way through the unknown west. When she was 12 years old, she was kidnapped by an enemy Native American tribe called the Hidatsa. Then, legend has it, the chief of the Hidatsa tribe sold Sacagawea into slavery.

In 1804, she became a translator and guide for a group of explorers led by Lewis and Clark. She helped them find their way from near the Dakotas to the Pacific Ocean. She became a famous Native American in our history for being brave and helping these men discover unknown territory.

Lewis and Clark Enlist Help

Sacagawea, also spelled Sacajawea, is best known for her role in helping Meriwether Lewis and William Clark during their journey to explore the American West. They set out on their journey on May 14, 1804. They left from near what is now Wood River, Illinois; but it was that winter in South Dakota when they met Sacagawea. They reached the Pacific Ocean on the coast of Oregon in November 1805.

A journey like this had never been done before. Now, we call this land the American West. In those days it was a new frontier full of unknown native people and dangerous land. Without the help of someone who knew the land, Lewis and Clark may not have made it to the Pacific.

Sacagawea was the young Shoshone wife of a French-Canadian fur trapper named Toussaint Charbonneau. Together, she and her husband served as interpreters, guides, and negotiators for Lewis and Clark. Their friendship with Clark was so strong that when they returned, they moved to his hometown of St. Louis. Clark even became the guardian of her children after her death.

127

Question Number: 91   RI.4.9

Which of the following sentences integrates information from both texts above?

Ⓐ Despite being kidnapped and sold into slavery at the age of 12, Sacagawea went on to guide and befriend Meriwether Lewis and William Clark on their journey of exploration from South Dakota to the Pacific Ocean in Oregon.

Ⓑ Sacagawea is a famous and brave Shoshone Indian who helped guide Lewis and Clark on their journey to find new territory.

Ⓒ Sacagawea developed such a strong bond with William Clark that after the expedition she moved to his city and even left her children in his care when she died.

Ⓓ Sacagawea was kidnapped by the Hidatsa in 1804.

Question Number: 92   RI.4.9

Which of the following sentences combines information from both texts above?

Ⓐ Sacagawea was a Shoshone princess who very slyly took charge of one of the most famous explorations in American History.

Ⓑ Sacagawea did serve as interpreter and guide, but it was merely her presence that showed William's and Clark's peaceful intentions when the expedition encountered new tribes.

Ⓒ At twelve, Sacagawea was kidnapped and sold to a French-Canadian man; but she eventually married that fur trapper, Toussaint Charbonneau, and together they be came part of an expedition that will live on in history.

Ⓓ Sacagawea was kidnapped by the Hidatsa in 1804.

Question Number: 93   RI.4.9

Which of the following sentences combines information from both texts above?

Ⓐ Sacagawea was a member of the Shoshone tribe of Native Americans.

Ⓑ Sacagawea was brave because she was kidnapped as a child, went on a treacherous and historic journey across the American West, and also ventured to live in a new city.

Ⓒ Sacagawea could not have aided the Lewis and Clark expedition without the help of her husband, who was an experienced fur trapper.

Ⓓ Sacagawea was kidnapped by the Hidatsa in 1804.

One Theory on Dinosaur Extinction

Have you ever thought about what happened to the dinosaurs that once roamed the Earth? Well, scientists have developed several ideas through the years. One idea is that a giant meteorite crashed into our planet and caused a huge dust cloud to cover the Earth. The dust cloud was so enormous that it kept the sun's rays from reaching Earth. This caused all of the plants to die. With nothing to eat, the herbivores died. Because of this, the large carnivores also died, leaving the planet with no dinosaurs.

Dinosaur Die-out: Competing Theories

There are many theories about how dinosaurs came to be extinct. Scientists do not all agree about what may have happened. The most recent idea says that a giant meteorite crashed into the earth. It kicked up enough dust and dirt that the Sun's rays did not reach Earth for a very long time. This prevented plants from making their own food via photosynthesis. In turn, plant-eaters died for lack of food. After that, meat-eaters followed.

The other leading idea says that dinosaurs died out when the Earth went through a time of volcanoes were erupting. Like the meteorite idea, it is thought that the volcanoes spewed enough ash into the air that the Sun's rays were blocked. This also caused plant and animal life to die.

Question Number: 94   **RI.4.9**

Which of the following paragraphs combines information from both of the above texts?

Ⓐ Dinosaurs are thought to have become extinct 65 million years ago, but some scientists theorize that they are still roaming remote parts of the Amazon Rainforest.

Ⓑ Dinosaurs became extinct because of widespread volcanic eruptions that blocked sunlight from reaching Earth. When this happened, plants died, beginning a disruption of the food chain that dinosaurs didn't survive.

Ⓒ One theory suggests a meteorite caused dinosaur extinction, while another claims widespread volcanic eruptions caused the animals to die. Both theories, however, center around the idea that plants did not get needed sunlight and plant-eating and meat-eating animals died as a result.

Ⓓ Scientists have argued for many years but finally agree a meteor crashing into Earth caused the dinosaurs to become extinct.

Question Number: 95   **RI.4.9**

Which of the following sentences combines information from both of the above texts?

Ⓐ   Several theories exist about how dinosaurs became extinct; but the two main theories are that either a meteorite crashing into Earth or a series of massive volcanic eruptions caused the animals to die out.

Ⓑ   Dinosaurs may have become extinct because a giant meteorite crashed into the Earth somewhere near the Gulf of Mexico, but scientists are not sure.

Ⓒ   If producers are unable to get sunlight, photosynthesis can't take place. This means plant-eating animals do not have food, thus meaning that meat-eating animals will not have food either.

Ⓓ   Herbivores and carnivores are both extinct because of volcanic eruptions.

End of Additional Questions

NOTES

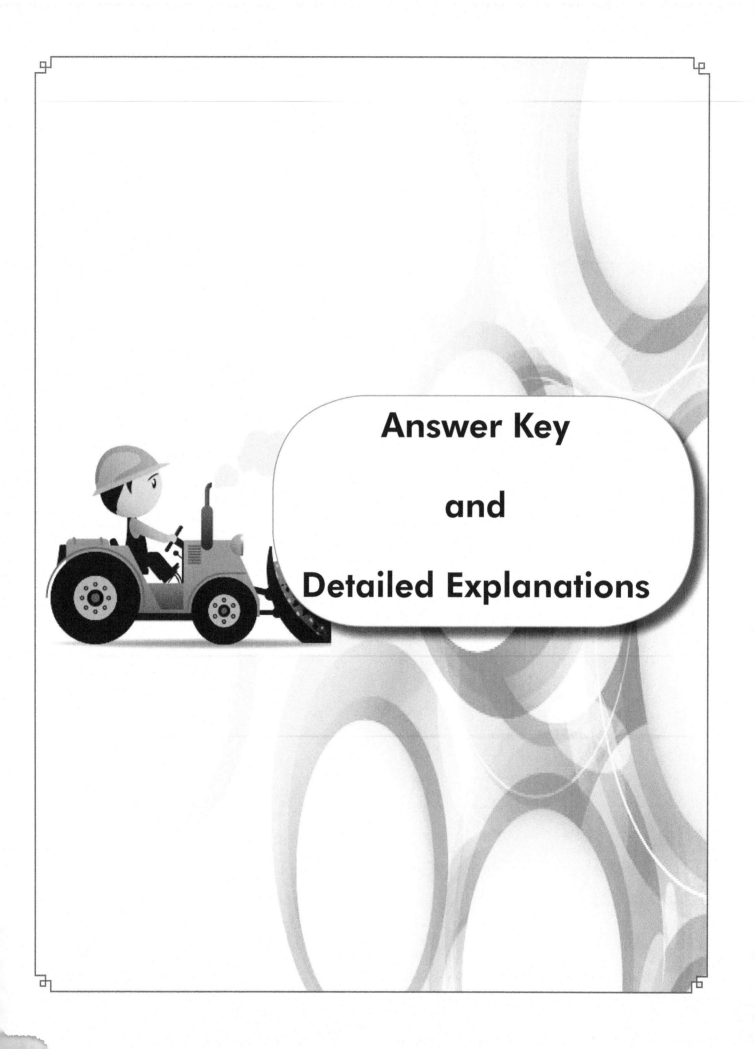

Answer Key

and

Detailed Explanations

Question No.	Answer	Detailed Explanations	CCSS
1	A	Ellie's father explains that her wings help her gather speed and go fast. Although option B is a fact from the story, it does not show how Ellie can run faster, but how she can stop fast.	RL.4.1
2	B	The second choice is correct, because the passage states that "You can also use them as brakes while turning and stopping." You refers to Ellie and other ostriches, and them refers to their wings.	RL.4.1
3	C	Choice C is correct, because cups and ornaments are objects that are useful to people. The first two choices are details describing the ostrich's size and the egg's weight.	RL.4.1
4	C	The third choice is correct. We know that the poet was surprised to hear a song from the shell, because the poet "listened hard, / And it was really true." When a person is surprised by something or can't believe it, it makes sense that they would gather more information before confirming that it is true.	RL.4.1
5	D	The fourth choice is correct. We can infer that Cindy did not like what her mother had cooked, because she asked if she could cook something else (the frozen pizza).	RL.4.1
6	C	The third choice is correct. We can infer that Ben and his dad were going to a mountain, because the passage says that there was a new blanket of snow outside. Also, his dad told him to grab his skis. Our background knowledge tells us that people ski on snow-covered mountains.	RL.4.1
7	C	The third choice is correct. We can infer that this takes place in the early morning at sunrise, because the sky was turning from dark to pinkish-yellow. We know that at nighttime, the sky is dark. We also know that it becomes light in the early morning.	RL.4.1
8	D	The fourth choice is correct. The author says she, "lay on the windowsill." These are things only a cat would do. The mention of birds in the 5th sentence is also a clue, because cats prey on birds.	RL.4.1
9	C	The third choice is correct. Rhonda's new school is different than her old one, but Rhonda liked the different things at her new school.	RL.4.2
10	D	The fourth choice is correct. Telling her little brother that she was sorry didn't make Polly's little brother feel better. Polly's little brother started to feel better when Polly read him a story.	RL.4.2

133

Question No.	Answer	Detailed Explanations	CCSS
11	C	The third choice is correct. Since Karen worked hard and completed her assignments on time, she received an A in the class.	RL.4.2
12	A	The first choice is correct. If Mr. Toad had shared his food, he wouldn't have been so full and would have been able to escape the hunter.	RL.4.2
13	C	The third choice is correct. Frank's classmates quit asking him to hang out, because all he wanted to do was quote information from books.	RL.4.2
14	C	The third choice is correct. If the monkey wasn't greedy and just let go of the cookies, his hand wouldn't be stuck in the cookie jar.	RL.4.2
15	B	The second choice is correct, because it tells only the important information from the passage. Option D also gives a summary, but it has additional information that is not needed.	RL.4.2
16	A	The first choice is correct. We know that Beau was anxious, because he was in a situation where most kids would be anxious. The passage also told us that he was fidgeting and playing with his button.	RL.4.3
17	C	The third choice is correct. Huckleberry Hound was on the porch at the beginning of the story. The first sentence of the passage tells us so.	RL.4.3
18	B	The second choice is correct. Huckleberry Hound chased the rabbit in the field. The second sentence of the passage tells us so.	RL.4.3
19	A	The first choice is correct. Huckleberry Hound was in the yard at the end of the story. The last sentence of the passage tells us so.	RL.4.3
20	C	The passages show that Mary was very shy and Timmy was not. Although option A is a correct statement, it does not describe how they felt about presenting.	RL.4.3
21	D	"Twinkled like diamonds" is a simile. A simile compares two things using like or as. The way the girl's eyes twinkle is being compared to how diamonds twinkle.	RL.4.4

Question No.	Answer	Detailed Explanations	CCSS
22	B	This is a metaphor. A metaphor is a direct comparison of 2 unlike objects. Her heart is being compared to stone. Stone is hard, and her heart was hard (meaning she was not very sensitive).	RL.4.4
23	C	This is a metaphor. The sound the bird made was being compared to music, meaning it made a pleasant, entertaining sound.	RL.4.4
24	D	Birds eat very little, and Suzy eats very little.	RL.4.4
25	B	A compass guides people in the right location. The man's wife guides him to the right paths in life.	RL.4.4
26	D	A lemon is sour and unpleasant. A car that doesn't run well is unpleasant.	RL.4.4
27	D	A simile compares two objects using like or as. This simile compares the hardness of the biscuits to the hardness of rocks.	RL.4.4
28	C	Angels are kind. Janice is kind.	RL.4.4
29	C	Oxen are strong. Jimmy is strong.	RL.4.4
30	B	A metaphor directly compares 2 unlike objects. Libby is being compared to a road hog.	RL.4.4
31	D	The Three Little Pigs is told in sequence or chronological order. That means that the events are told in the order that they happened.	RL.4.5
32	D	Descriptive texts tell the characteristics of a particular subject.	RL.4.5
33	D	Problem/Solution texts start out explaining a problem. Then, they offer a solution. The problem in this passage is that Beau wanted a dog. The solution was for him to keep his room clean.	RL.4.5
34	A	When an author adds descriptions about characters' emotions and feelings, it allows the reader to connect more deeply with the characters.	RL.4.5
35	C	Descriptive text is about a particular topic in no specific order. That is the type of text used in this passage.	RL.4.5

Question No.	Answer	Detailed Explanations	CCSS
36	B	Second person point of view is when the writer is talking directly to the reader.	RL.4.6
37	B	Second person point of view is when the writer is speaking directly to the reader.	RL.4.6
38	C	Third person point of view is when the story is being told by someone who is not a character in the story.	RL.4.6
39	A	First person point of view is when one of the characters in the story is telling the story. Pronouns such as I and me are used.	RL.4.6
40	A	First person point of view is when the story is being told by one of the characters in the story. Pronouns such as I and me are used.	RL.4.6
41	C	The third choice is correct, because it is about baby monkeys. There are baby monkeys in the picture.	RL.4.7
42	C	The third choice is correct, because it is about a kitten at a construction site. The kitten in the picture is in a concrete pipe.	RL.4.7
43	C	The third choice is correct, because it is about singing. The girl in the picture is holding a microphone and singing.	RL.4.7
44	D	The fourth choice is correct, because it is about a sandcastle shaped like a dragon.	RL.4.7
45	B	The passage is about a way that a teacher helps a student learn to read. A photo of a teacher and a student with a book would be appropriate.	RL.4.7
46	D	Although each description of images could be found in the story, only option D describes the moral of the story. When the friend walks away without giving advice, the man reminds him he made need advice someday too.	RL.4.7
47	C	The illustration is from the book Treasure Island where the young boy is saying goodbye to his mother. The hug and the look on the boy's face help the reader determine this is a goodbye hug filled with much longing.	RL.4.7

Question No.	Answer	Detailed Explanations	CCSS
48	A	A Venn Diagram allows the reader to list out characteristics or details of the story to determine if there are any overlapping ideas. In the case of these two passages, both students clearly loved writing, even if they had different approaches to sharing their story. Because we did not read the stories, we do not know if they were fiction.	RL.4.7
49	B	Option B is the closest image to what Timmy could show to add depth to his story. The reader does not know much about his story other than it involves a spaceship. It does not mention an elephant; that is Mary's story. It does not mention a boy playing soccer. Option D shows a student who is raising his hand, possibly in excitement like Timmy; however, that does not add depth to his story, just the paragraph describing his day.	RL.4.7
50	C	The third choice is correct, because it tells a way that the two boys are alike. Comparing means telling how one or more subjects are alike.	RL.4.9
51	D	To contrast means to tell how two subjects are different. The fourth choice tells what Stanley likes to do and what Timothy likes to do.	RL.4.9
52	A	The first choice is correct. Both boys volunteer at the recycling center.	RL.4.9
53	B	The second choice is correct, because it tells how each aunt dresses. The story specifically describes how the two Aunt's dress.	RL.4.9
54	A	The first choice is correct, because it tells what kind of car each aunt drives. The story specifically describes the types of vehicles the two Aunts drive.	RL.4.9
55	C	The third choice is correct, because it tells what happened to the animals after the restaurant opened. The different animals all had various complaints.	RL.4.9
56	A	The first choice is correct, because it told what happened to the birds and to the beavers.	RL.4.9

Question No.	Answer	Detailed Explanations	CCSS
57	D	The fourth answer choice is correct because it mentions the advantage to getting friends to join. While the third answer choice does mention getting friends to join, it does not mention any benefit that would encourage the audience to recruit their friends.	RI.4.1
58	D	The second answer choice is correct. Paragraph 2 includes details like, "when the weather begins to get warmer after winter, these little frogs start to sing," and their song, "can be heard for miles around." Paragraph 3 also helps support her point by including details about how spring peepers "hide under fallen leaves or even in a small hole in the ground," when cold weather comes. Singing would make the peeper easy to find, while hiding would make it difficult to see one.	RI.4.1
59	A	The first choice is correct, because it is the main idea of the passage.	RI.4.2
60	C	Dumping large amounts of trash from factories and houses affects the soil according to the passage.	RI.4.2
61	C	The word repaid is a context clue that helps us figure out what reimbursed means.	RI.4.4
62	D	Boycott means refuse to buy something. In this case, the people would refuse to go to a store.	RI.4.4
63	B	The second sentence tells us exactly the definition of copra.	RI.4.4
64	C	Favorable means positive. People enjoyed it is a clue.	RI.4.4
65	D	The text structure is sequence, because the steps are given in the order that they are supposed to occur.	RI.4.5
66	D	This is persuasive writing, because it gives an opinion and tries to get others to agree.	RI.4.5
67	A	This is a comparative essay because it is looking at the issue of cell phones in schools from two different perspectives: elementary and middle.	RI.4.5
68	A	This is a comparison essay because it gives both sides of the discussion of school uniforms. It compares the pros and the cons.	RI.4.5

Question No.	Answer	Detailed Explanations	CCSS
69	D	The fourth choice is correct. The first hand account is by the baton twirler and is limited to her personal experiences and observations. The second hand account covers the observations about the entire parade by the reporter.	RI.4.6
70	D	The fourth choice is correct. There is information in both texts about the weather, the marching band, the baton twirlers, and the crowd. The other answer choices only appear in one of the two accounts.	RI.4.6
71	A	The first choice is correct. We learn in the firsthand account that the narrator is embarrassed by the events during the parade, while the secondhand account omits emotions and includes mostly facts about the parade.	RI.4.6
72	C	The third choice is correct. The firsthand account describes how bunches of people walked down the street on their way to the inauguration, and the secondhand account gives details about the inauguration on that same day.	RI.4.6
73	D	The fourth choice is correct. The other answer choices have no support.	RI.4.6
74	A	The first choice is correct. It could be argued that the details in both accounts are important, and the third and fourth choices are false.	RI.4.6
75	C	The third choice is correct. The firsthand account is a letter from John Glenn himself to then President Bill Clinton. The secondhand account gives information about John Glenn's 1998 return mission to space.	RI.4.6
76	A	The first choice is correct. It is the only information to appear in both documents.	RI.4.6
77	A	The first choice is correct. It explains how the two texts are different.	RI.4.6
78	B	The second choice is correct. Firsthand accounts represent people's personal experiences, while secondhand accounts are told or written by those who gather the information about the event from another source.	RI.4.6

Question No.	Answer	Detailed Explanations	CCSS
79	A	The first choice is correct. Steps in a process would be most easily understood with the help of a numbered, illustrated list of steps. A timeline is meant to cover a longer time span, and a map would not help the reader understand steps in a process.	RI.4.7
80	C	The third choice is correct. Camping is the only topic listed that would require knowledge of tents like the ones pictured.	RI.4.7
81	C	The third answer choice is correct. The photographs show the different stages of a caterpillar going into its chrysalis in preparation to become a butterfly. The captions use words like, "change" and "transition" to make that more clear.	RI.4.7
82	D	Yellow teeth is a specific example of how smoking affects the way one looks.	RI.4.8
83	B	Choice 3 is how onions can make you smell bad, not cigarettes.	RI.4.8
84	A	Choice 1 has nothing to do with driving.	RI.4.8
85	B	Don't Let Toads Disappear is an appropriate title, because the purpose of the text is to encourage people to do things to prevent toads from vanishing.	RI.4.8
86	D	The fourth answer choice is correct. The first three choices include only information from one of the texts. The fourth choice integrates information from both texts.	RI.4.9
87	B	The second choice is correct. Information from the other three choices are not found in the texts.	RI.4.9
88	A	The first choice is correct. This is the only choice with a pair of sentences from each text that mean essentially the same thing. When doing research, one should look for similar information found in multiple texts, as this adds to its validity.	RI.4.9
89	A	The first choice is correct. It integrates information from both texts about the growth and length of a peacock's feathers.	RI.4.9
90	D	The fourth choice is correct. It is the only answer choice that includes information from both texts.	RI.4.9

Question No.	Answer	Detailed Explanations	CCSS
91	A	Only the first choice includes information from both texts. Choice 2 only uses information from the first passage, while choice 3 only uses information from the second passage.	RI.4.9
92	C	The third choice is correct. The first choice is untrue, and the second choice includes information not mentioned in either text above.	RI.4.9
93	B	The second choice is correct. It uses examples from both texts to justify bravery as a character trait for Sacagawea. The first choice is a statement of fact, rather than an integration of facts from multiple texts. The third choice is an opinion not represented in either text.	RI.4.9
94	C	The third choice is correct. The first choice is untrue, and the second choice asserts the volcano theory as fact, disregarding any discussion of a meteorite.	RI.4.9
95	A	The first choice is correct. It integrates information from both texts. The second choice gives additional information on only one theory, and the third choice further explains how blocked sunlight could result in dinosaur extinction.	RI.4.9

Common Core Standards Cross-reference Table

CCSS	Standard Description	Page No./ Question No.
RL.4.1	Refer to details and examples in a text when explaining what the text says explicitly and when drawing inferences from the text.	
RL.4.2	Determine a theme of a story, drama, or poem from details in the text; summarize the text.	
RL.4.3	Describe in depth a character, setting, or event in a story or drama, drawing on specific details in the text (e.g., a character's thoughts, words, or actions).	
RL.4.4	Determine the meaning of words and phrases as they are used in a text, including those that allude to significant characters found in mythology (e.g., Herculean).	
RL.4.5	Explain major differences between poems, drama, and prose, and refer to the structural elements of poems (e.g., verse, rhythm, meter) and drama (e.g., casts of characters, settings, descriptions, dialogue, stage directions) when writing or speaking about a text.	
RL.4.6	Compare and contrast the point of view from which different stories are narrated, including the difference between first- and third-person narrations.	
RL.4.7	Make connections between the text of a story or drama and a visual or oral presentation of the text, identifying where each version reflects specific descriptions and directions in the text.	
RL.4.9	Compare and contrast the treatment of similar themes and topics (e.g., opposition of good and evil) and patterns of events (e.g., the quest) in stories, myths, and traditional literature from different cultures.	
RI.4.1	Refer to details and examples in a text when explaining what the text says explicitly and when drawing inferences from the text.	
RI.4.2	Determine the main idea of a text and explain how it is supported by key details; summarize the text.	
RI.4.3	Explain events, procedures, ideas, or concepts in a historical, scientific, or technical text, including what happened and why, based on specific information in the text.	

CCSS	Standard Description	Page No./ Question No.
RI.4.4	Determine the meaning of general academic and domain-specific words or phrases in a text relevant to a grade 4 topic or subject area.	
RI.4.5	Describe the overall structure (e.g., chronology, comparison, cause/effect, problem/solution) of events, ideas, concepts, or information in a text or part of a text.	
RI.4.6	Compare and contrast a firsthand and secondhand account of the same event or topic; describe the differences in focus and the information provided.	
RI.4.7	Interpret information presented visually, orally, or quantitatively (e.g., in charts, graphs, diagrams, time lines, animations, or interactive elements on Web pages) and explain how the information contributes to an understanding of the text in which it appears.	
RI.4.8	Explain how an author uses reasons and evidence to support particular points in a text.	
RI.4.9	Integrate information from two texts on the same topic in order to write or speak about the subject knowledgeably.	

Online Resources

CCSS	URL	QR Code
RL.4.1	LumosLearning.com/a/15089	
RL.4.1	LumosLearning.com/a/15090	
RL.4.2	LumosLearning.com/a/15091	
RL.4.2	LumosLearning.com/a/15093	
RL.4.3	LumosLearning.com/a/15092	

CCSS	URL	QR Code
RL.4.3	LumosLearning.com/a/15094	
RL.4.3	LumosLearning.com/a/15095	
RL.4.4	LumosLearning.com/a/15096	
RL.4.5	LumosLearning.com/a/15097	
RL.4.6	LumosLearning.com/a/15098	

CCSS	URL	QR Code
RL.4.7	LumosLearning.com/a/15099	
RL.4.9	LumosLearning.com/a/15100	
RI.4.1	LumosLearning.com/a/15105	
RI.4.2	LumosLearning.com/a/15101	
RI.4.3	LumosLearning.com/a/15106	

CCSS	URL	QR Code
RI.4.4	LumosLearning.com/a/15102	
RI.4.5	LumosLearning.com/a/15103	
RI.4.6	LumosLearning.com/a/15107	
RI.4.7	LumosLearning.com/a/15108	
RI.4.8	LumosLearning.com/a/15104	

CCSS	URL	QR Code
RI.4.9	LumosLearning.com/a/15109	

NOTES

 **Test Prep and Smart Homework Help**

Lumos StepUp is a unique e-Learning program that provides online resources along with personalized coaching to help improve student achievement.

 Practice Assessments that mirror standardized Tests

 Parent Portal: Review online work of your child

 Individualized homework assistance (StepUp® Coach™)

 Student Portal: Anywhere access to Learning Resources

 Master Tech Enhanced Question Types

 Discover Educational Apps, Books, and Videos

Subscribe Now ▶

 888-309-8227

 www.lumoslearning.com/stepup

Other Books in SkillBuilder Series

English Language and Grammar SkillBuilder

- Conventions
- Vocabulary
- Knowledge of Language

Operations and Algebraic Thinking SkillBuilder

- Real World Problems
- Multi-Step Problems

Fractions and Base Ten SkillBuilder

- Place Value
- Compare Numbers
- Compare Fractions

Measurement, Representation, Interpretation and Geometry SkillBuilder

- Units of Measurement
- Angle Measurement
- Classifying Plane

http://lumoslearning.com/a/sbtb